IN·HONOUR·BOUND

MOUNTBATTEN

Eighty years in pictures

Macmillan

First published 1979
by MACMILLAN LONDON LIMITED
London and Basingstoke
Associated Companies in Delhi, Dublin, Hong Kong,
Johannesburg, Lagos, Melbourne, New York, Singapore & Tokyo

This book was designed and produced by
GEORGE RAINBIRD LTD
36 Park Street, London W1Y 4DE

Mountbatten, eighty years in pictures.
    1. Mountbatten, Louis, *Earl Mountbatten*,
    b. 1900 – Portraits, etc.
    I. Mountbatten, Louis, *Earl Mountbatten*,
    b. 1900
    941.082'092"4   DA89.1.M59

ISBN 0–333–26558–0

Designer: Trevor Vincent
Photography: Derrick Witty

Colour originated by Gilchrist Bros. Ltd, Leeds, West Yorkshire.
Printed and bound by Jarrold and Sons Limited, Norwich

Frontispiece:
Mountbatten at Classiebawn,
his Irish Castle.

Contents

Foreword

I have always refused to authorize any biography during my lifetime and I certainly never intended to write any memoirs myself. However, in 1967 I did agree to the television series about my Life and Times, and much of the personal film I had collected over the years was used. This was a great success and has been shown in over forty countries, and in some several times over, and I personally dubbed it into both French and German.

In recent years I have spent a considerable amount of time sorting out the thousands of photographs I have amassed in my Archives, and from time to time have enlisted the help of some of my personal friends to help with the task of putting them into albums in some sort of order.

Several of them remarked that it was a great pity that such a large number of these photographs would never be made public and suggested I should consider allowing another series of my Life and Times, this time in still-life pictures. They pointed out that even though a biography of my life may be produced after my death, it would only be possible to include a fraction of my personal photographs, and in any case the photographs themselves would be infinitely more interesting if I were to describe the events behind them.

I somewhat reluctantly agreed to consider the possibility and as I went into it in greater depth I soon realized I had such a vast number of photographs covering the past seventy-nine years that there would certainly be no problem in producing a pictorial view of my lifetime; the great difficulty would be in deciding which photographs to leave out.

This is not, of course, a complete biography in pictures but I have personally selected those pictures which I hope will give an insight into the many varied, interesting and sometimes historic events in which I have been involved.

What I thought would be a chore has turned out to be a task which has given me tremendous pleasure. There can be few people who have not enjoyed the fun of turning the pages of a family album. I hope that some of them will enjoy turning the pages of mine.

Finally, I would like to express my thanks to my Secretary, John Barratt, who has done invaluable research for the captions to the photographs, and to my archivist, Mrs Mollie Travis.

Mountbatten of Burma

A.F.

A Royal Childhood

Dickie in the arms of his great-grandmother, Queen Victoria, after his christening on 17 July 1900.

THE British genealogist, Sir Ian Moncrieff has written of the Mountbattens: 'There can hardly be another family in Europe so well documented over so long a span of time, for the Mountbattens belong to the oldest traceable Protestant ruling house in the world.'

Their line can be traced without any doubt back to the ninth century and to Charlemagne. At that time their lands were in Brabant and Lorraine and it was not until the thirteenth century that the son of the reigning Duke of Brabant inherited the Principality of Hesse where his descendants continued to rule until 1918.

The family grew steadily in strength and stature. In 1529 Philip I of Hesse drew up the original Protest from which the Protestant religion drew its name. It was Grand Duke Louis I, confirmed in his title after the Napoleonic wars, who gave Hesse such an important place among the German States and who ensured that Darmstadt played a leading role in Germany's industrial revolution.

His son Grand Duke Louis II was the father of Marie and Alexander. Marie married the future Tsar Alexander II of Russia and her brother Alexander accompanied her to Russia. He was decorated for gallantry in the war against the Caucasian rebel Shamyl but on his return eloped with his sister's attractive Lady-in-Waiting, Countess Julie of Hauke. This was a morganatic marriage made against the wishes of the Tsar who dismissed him from the Russian army. Alexander then entered the service of the Emperor of Austria where he distinguished himself particularly in the Battle of Solferino and won three more decorations for gallantry; clearly an outstanding and courageous soldier.

Julie was created Princess of Battenberg and so Prince Alexander's eldest son became Prince Louis of Battenberg. In 1868, at the age of fourteen, encouraged by Queen Victoria's son Alfred, Duke of Edinburgh, who was serving in the Royal Navy, and her daughter Alice, who had married Grand Duke Louis IV, Prince Louis became a naturalized British subject and entered the Royal Navy.

In 1884 he married his cousin Victoria, the eldest daughter of the Grand Duke Louis IV of Hesse and the Grand Duchess Alice, Queen Victoria's second daughter. Alice died from diphtheria at the early age of thirty-five on 14 December 1878 and Queen Victoria thereafter took a special interest in her Hessian grandchildren. She was particularly attached to her granddaughter Victoria who at the age of fifteen took on the task of acting as hostess for her father, and mother to her four sisters and two brothers. Queen Victoria often had them to stay at Windsor, Osborne, Balmoral and sometimes Buckingham Palace. (Her regular and delightful correspondence with her granddaughter was edited by Richard Hough and published as *Advice to a Granddaughter*.)

Princess Louis had been born on 5 April 1863 in the Lancaster Tower of Windsor Castle where she also gave birth, twenty-three years later, to her eldest daughter Alice. Alice married Prince Andrew of Greece and was the present Duke of Edinburgh's mother. Prince and Princess Louis' younger daughter Louise married King Gustaf VI Adolf of Sweden, and their elder son George, who had a brilliant brain, entered the Royal Navy but died in 1938.

George's younger brother, named Louis like his father, was born at 6 a.m. on 25 June 1900 at Frogmore House, Windsor in the sixty-third year of Queen Victoria's reign. After his birth Queen Victoria specially asked that the name Albert should be added to the four others and he was christened Louis Francis Albert Victor Nicholas. The family had a meeting to decide which of these five Christian names he would be called by. It could not be Louis, which would be confusing as this was his father's name. Nicky was suggested but Tsar Nicholas II, his father's first cousin who had married his mother's sister Alexandra, was called Nicky in the family, so they decided to call him Dickie.

The announcement of Dickie's birth was printed in the Court Circular under the heading of 'Windsor Castle'. Queen Victoria agreed to be his Godmother and more or less took charge of his christening. It was organized by the Queen's own Court officials and held at Frogmore House when Dickie was three weeks old.

The christening was held on 17 July 1900 in a large drawing-room on the ground floor, especially converted for the occasion. The day was hot and servants were instructed to put buckets filled with ice under the chairs of the principal participants. The Queen drove in her landau the short distance from Windsor Castle, and although she was rather crippled and blind, she insisted on holding the big baby throughout the ceremony. The infant showed early signs of obstreperousness by knocking off the Queen's spectacles with one hand and entangling his other arm in her cap-veil at the font; but the Queen bore this calmly and noted afterwards: 'He is a beautiful large child and behaved very well.'

In November 1900 the family moved into a rented house in London, 4 Hans Crescent, and on 11 January Prince and Princess Louis were summoned to Osborne, where Queen Victoria was dying at the age of eighty-one. The Victorian age was over; Dickie, six months younger than the new century, was himself to play a large part in the shattering events of its central decades.

For the first ten years of his life Dickie was educated mainly by his mother and she did it very well, instilling a love of work and accuracy and ready to discuss frankly any subject that came up. He spent a lot of

Dickie in his mother's arms. July 1900.

time with her when his father was away, and accompanied her on some of her many travels; though this could have been a disruptive or limited education for a small boy, it was exactly the opposite, for she was a remarkable, to some people formidable, woman with a great deal of wisdom as well as a strong character. She took up many subjects with enthusiasm, not in a superficial manner but pursuing them as far as she possibly could. She became an authority on archaeology, and thought deeply about politics, psychology and the technological miracles that took place in her lifetime.

Like her grandmother, Queen Victoria, she was intensely interested in all her relations and was a loving mother to her four children, encouraging them with letters when apart, and taking a great deal of care over their moral education and the development of their characters.

Dickie's life also contained regular holidays, often with his relations abroad. As has already been mentioned, his mother's sister, Alix, was married to Tsar Nicholas II of Russia, who was his father's first cousin, but another of his mother's sisters, Elizabeth (Aunt Ella) had married the Tsar's uncle, the Grand Duke Serge. Dickie spent idyllic holidays with his Russian cousins, both in Germany and in the autumnal splendour of the Russian court. In July 1901 the family visited Grand Duke and Grand Duchess Serge at Ilinskoe, their country house near Moscow, then going on to Peterhof, one of the lovely Imperial Palaces near St Petersburg.

HMS *Implacable*, 1901. Sitting on chairs: 4. Princess Alice, 5. Prince Louis as a Captain, 6. Princess Louis with Dickie on her lap, 7. Princess Louise, 8. Miss Nona Kerr (Lady-in-Waiting), 9. Her brother Commander Mark Kerr. Sitting on the deck at Prince Louis' feet, his elder son George.

The Grand Duke of Hesse and the Rhine (Uncle Ernie), with his four sisters and their husbands after the marriage of Dickie's sister Alice to Prince Andrew of Greece in 1903. Left to right: Uncle Ernie, the Tsarina and Tsar Nicholas II (Alix and Nicky), Princess and Prince Henry of Prussia (Irene and Harry), Princess Elizabeth (Ella) and Grand Duke Serge, the Tsar's uncle, and Dickie's parents, Princess Victoria and Prince Louis of Battenberg.

Dickie's first ride on a pony held by Marie Pavlovna, Grand Duke Serge's niece, at Ilinskoe, Serge's house near Moscow, 1901.

The Russian Imperial Family in 1906. Left to right: Anastasia, Alexei (the Tsarevitch), Marie, the Tsarina, the Tsar, Olga and (seated) Tatiana.

The Tsar and Tsarina in traditional Russian Imperial robes for a costume ball.

The Tsar, Dickie's Uncle Nicky, was a simple, kind-hearted man who liked nothing better than to be at home playing with his children, but was unfortunately rather weak and indecisive – a character that fitted unhappily with his position as absolute monarch, Tsar of All the Russias.

In 1904 the Grand Duke Serge was blown to pieces by a bomb thrown by a nihilist in Moscow, where he was Governor; a grim foretaste of what was to come for the other members of the Imperial Family. His wife Elizabeth sold all her vast possessions and founded the first Nursing Sisters' Movement in Russia, the Order of St Martha and St Mary, and came to be loved and revered in Russia almost as a saint. The last time Dickie saw his uncle Serge was at the wedding of his sister, Alice, to Prince Andrew of Greece in Darmstadt in 1903. Alice had a daughter, Margarita, in 1905 and a second daughter, Theodora (known in the family as Dolla) in 1906, the elder sisters of the present Duke of Edinburgh. The two little girls, though Dickie's nieces, were not much younger than him.

The Battenberg family in 1902. Louise, Prince Louis, Alice (at back), Princess Louis, Dickie, Georgie.

Left to right: 1. Grand Duke of Hesse and the Rhine and his daughter Elizabeth, Grand Duchess Serge, Princess Henry of Prussia, 2. Georgie, Prince Louis, Grand Duke Serge, Bobby (Prince Sigismund, son of Princess Henry of Prussia), 3. Princess Louis with Dickie, his sisters Louise and Alice, Princess Henry of Prussia with her son Henry, 1902.

Dickie holding his niece, Princess Margarita of Greece (Prince Philip's sister), Heiligenberg, 1905.

Dickie's beloved teddy bear, 'Sonnenbein', 70 Cadogan Square, 1905.

Other holidays were spent at his father's castle in Hesse, Schloss Heiligenberg. Here, aged two, he began to learn to ride (though his first ride in a pannier on a pony had actually been at Ilinskoe), caught his first glimpse of travelling entertainers, which fired him with a lifelong love of the circus, and went tobogganing in the winter with his brother and sisters. At the age of five, he was introduced to the thrill of hearing his own voice on a new form of phonograph with wax cylinders and was quite unable to recognize it! In 1906 the children went to stay with

Dickie aged 3 at Sopwell,
St Albans

Dickie, aged 3, Georgie, aged
11, in the Conservatory at
Sopwell.

Princess Elizabeth of Hesse
(Dickie's first cousin) had this
little house specially built for her
in the garden at Wolfsgarten. In
this photograph taken in 1903
are (left to right): Louise, Dickie,
Princess Elizabeth and Georgie.

their mother's brother, Grand Duke Ernest-Louis of Hesse and the
Rhine (Uncle Ernie), at Schloss Wolfsgarten, where he had built a little
house in the grounds for his daughter Elizabeth. Lord Mountbatten still
visits the last family home at Wolfsgarten when he can, to enjoy its
beauty and remember the idyllic atmosphere of a world that has utterly
disappeared.

The family also had holidays in England. The summer of 1903 was
spent at an attractive country house near St Albans called Sopwell. It
was here that Dickie celebrated his third birthday. One of the first of
many pets was given him for his birthday, a canary, so tame it could be
safely left outside its cage. Alas, one of Dickie's first memories was of
trying to pick up the little bird, losing his balance, and crushing it. In
the years that followed there was a succession of beloved pets: Scamp, a
black mongrel (a present from Great-Aunt Louise), white rabbits, and
as a seventh birthday present, a lamb, Millie. She was not always
obedient so Dickie put a cord with a running noose round her neck and
pulled hard when she would not come. When he saw that he was
choking her, he transferred the noose to her leg but when he pulled
hard she still used to make choking noises!

Dickie with his pet lamb, Millie, at Schloss Heiligenberg, 1904.

Like most small boys Dickie had lots of pets at one time or another, including white rabbits. Kendals, near Radlett, 1904.

Aged 4, at Kendals with a toy dog.

Opposite page: top left
Prince Louis of Battenberg, Mountbatten's father.

Opposite page: top right
A portrait of Mountbatten by Carlos Sancha.

Opposite page: bottom
Painted at his prep-school.

NAVAL REVIEW
June 1911.

JF Rathway.

ХРИСТОСЪ ВОСКРЕСЕ !

Съ праздникомъ
Св. Пасхи

СЪ РОЖДЕСТВОМЪ ХРИСТОВЫМЪ.

He and the family spent Christmas 1904 in the Isle of Wight with Princess Henry of Battenberg at Osborne Cottage. Princess Henry was Queen Victoria's youngest daughter, Beatrice, and thus Dickie's great-aunt, but she had married Prince Louis' brother, Prince Henry of Battenberg (Liko), making her also Dickie's aunt by marriage. She had succeeded her husband as Governor of the Isle of Wight, after he died of malaria on the Ashanti Expedition of 1896. This was an appointment her young nephew/great-nephew was later to hold.

Aged 4, at Kendals.

Left
Mountbatten as a child exchanged cards at Easter and Christmas with his Russian cousins. (These are the reverse of the cards reproduced on pages 36 and 37.)

A fancy dress party, Malta 1908. Prince Louis and Dickie in the centre are wearing costumes given them by the Tsar. Prince Louis is dressed as an Imperial Falconer, Dickie as a Cossack. Left to right: Lt Wells, Archie Savory, Prince Louis, Dickie, Lt Drummond and Captain Savory.

His father's job entailed some enjoyable travelling for Dickie. In 1901 Prince Louis commanded the fine new battleship *Implacable* at Malta and the family lived there with him until April the following year. In 1907 they returned to Malta when Prince Louis was made Second-in-Command of the Mediterranean Fleet. Dickie enjoyed himself immensely, especially at the parties. At one party he and his father wore costumes given them by Tsar Nicholas; Dickie went as a Cossack, his father as an Imperial Falconer.

Two years earlier, Christmas 1905 had been spent in Gibraltar, where Prince Louis was commanding the Second Cruiser Squadron, flying his Flag in HMS *Drake*. The family stayed at the Grand Hotel in Main Street. It was a great thrill for the young boy to watch the fortress being closed at sunset every evening, as one of the Garrison regiments beat the retreat with drums and bugles and marched through the streets with the great key to lock the fortress, marshalling before them the Spaniards who had to go outside Gibraltar to sleep. One splendid Christmas present had been from the Tsar, a uniform of the crack Russian Chevalier Garde, complete with helmet, breast-plate, boots, spurs and sword.

Prince Louis on board HMS *Drake* with his two sons, Dickie and Georgie, a naval cadet at the Royal Naval College, Osborne. Gibraltar 1905.

Prince Louis and his family settled in Valletta at 52 Strada Mezzodi (now South Street). Here outside the house are Dolla and Margarita in their Uncle Dickie's Maltese flat cart drawn by his donkey, Carolina.

Below: far left
Dickie on the mole at which the *Drake* was lying.

Below: left
Dickie playing with a toy snake. Behind him his father is talking to one of his staff.

Right
Drake visited Venice in 1906 and Dickie took his father paddling on the Lido beach.

Dickie in cuirass and helmet of the Chevalier Garde (the crack Household Cavalry of the Russian Empire), given to him by the Tsar for Christmas 1905. Dickie's grandfather, Prince Alexander of Hesse, was colonel of this regiment.

Early in 1906 Prince Louis took his whole family to Malaga on board his flagship, the *Drake*. Dickie remained on board with his nurse while the rest of the party went to Granada for two days; he was very pleased to be left behind on board and took to hitting the big drum on its stand on the half-deck as hard as he could, then running away. He loved ships and anything to do with them and was a great success with the men of his father's flagship. One officer remembers: 'He was a sore trial to me, for if he was not up aloft, he was down in the stokehold getting as black as a sweep and he would have fallen overboard and been drowned several times over except that I detailed a specially chosen able seaman to act as his dry-nurse.'

In March 1906 Dickie went with his family to Venice to see his father while he was there on board the *Drake*. His father took him for a picnic on the Lido and, while the party was being towed to land in a 27-foot whaler, the boat broached-to in the high wind and sea. But this frightening experience did not diminish Dickie's enthusiasm to join the Navy. In 1905 his brother Georgie had entered the Royal Naval College at Osborne and took every opportunity of wearing his cadet's uniform when home on leave. Dickie adored his brother and was determined to emulate him.

Princess Louis' brother Ernie, Grand Duke of Hesse, was keenly interested in aviation and provided Dickie with his first experiences of flying. In 1906 he arranged for a Parsifal airship to come to his country seat, Wolfsgarten, and take the family up. Dickie, barely six, was considered too young to fly but at the last moment more ballast was needed and Uncle Ernie reached out of the gondola and dragged Dickie aboard by his collar. In 1909, Dickie visited the first international exhibition of airships and aeroplanes in Frankfurt with his mother. She noted: 'All the flying machines had much trouble in leaving the ground and did not fly very far or high, but they were very manageable and dived under ropes stretched between high poles.'

From the end of May until mid-August 1908 Dickie was in Russia with his mother. They started off with a visit to his Aunt Ella, the Grand Duchess Serge of Russia, in the Nicholas Palace in the Kremlin. His nursery windows were on the second floor opposite the great bell, Kolokol, which had fallen from the belfry and had a chip knocked out of it and was then used as a chapel. At the other end of the Square opposite the Palace, there was a colossal gun known as Tsar Pushka. Also staying at the Palace was a cousin, the Grand Duke Dimitri, and Dickie made great friends with him, a friendship which lasted for the rest of the Grand Duke's life. He was one of the two conspirators who assassinated Rasputin and Dickie also got to know quite well the other conspirator, Prince Felix Yousoupoff.

Dickie's Uncle Ernie, Grand Duke of Hesse and the Rhine, an enthusiastic early aviator, provided the six-year-old boy's first taste of air travel in this airship which landed near Wolfsgarten. 1906.

On the courtyard steps of Schloss Heiligenberg are Princess Louise (Dickie's sister) with their niece Princess Theodora (Dolla) on her lap. Beside her Dickie, aged 7, and Dolla's elder sister Princess Margarita.

Dickie with a local Russian friend.

Dickie visited his Russian cousins
in 1908. Part of the holiday was
spent at Hapsal, a seaside resort
on the Baltic. Here at Villa
Brevern is (left to right): Louise,
Miss Nona Kerr, Lady-in-
Waiting to Princess Louis,
Grand Duke Dimitri Pavlovitch,
(Aunt Ella's nephew and one of
the two conspirators who
assassinated Rasputin), Dickie
and his mother.

Dickie with his mother near Hapsal.

Dickie in a field of daisies
near Hapsal.

30

Dickie bathing in the Baltic with his mother and Louise.

Right
Grand Duchess Marie of Russia whom Dickie, as a small boy, hoped to marry.

Yachting on the Baltic.

Dickie with one of his Russian cousins on the balustrade in front of the family villa in the Alexandrine Park.

In June the whole party went up to St Petersburg where they stayed in the Grand Duke Serge's palace. Then Princess Louis and her young son accompanied the Grand Duchess on a visit to Hapsal, a seaside resort on the Baltic. In August, they left Hapsal for Reval and then spent a week at Peterhof with the Tsar and Tsarina and their five children, Olga, Tatiana, Marie, Anastasia and Alexei, the haemophiliac Tsarevitch, at their villa in the Alexandrine Park, well away from the main palace. Dickie was attracted by the beauty of Marie who was one year older than himself, and vowed that when they grew up he would marry her. He still keeps a picture of her in his bedroom.

Princess Louis and Dickie returned to Heiligenberg on 11 August 1908 and her other son, George, joined them from Dartmouth for the summer holidays. The family had been looking forward to going back to the Mediterranean but Prince Louis was then appointed Commander-in-Chief of the Atlantic Fleet, based mainly at Dover.

Prince Andrew of Greece,
Dickie's brother-in-law and
Prince Philip's father, is holding
his eldest daughter Margarita.
Dickie makes faces between
his legs.

Dolla and Margarita with their
Uncle Dickie at Heiligenberg.

Dickie remained at Heiligenberg until 6 April 1909 when he went with his mother and family to Dover to see his father on board his flagship, the *Prince of Wales*.

After that the family paid visits to their two aunts, Princess Louise, Duchess of Argyll, and Princess Beatrice at Kensington Palace and, after a brief visit to Dover again in May, returned to Kensington Palace where Dickie developed chicken pox and had to be isolated in one wing of the Palace. In June Princess Louis and the children returned to Heiligenberg, as Prince Louis was going to be at sea for some time, and at the end of the month she sent Dickie and his sister Louise to Hemmelmark, the newly-built country house of Prince and Princess Henry of Prussia (Uncle Harry and Aunt Irene), while she paid a visit to Russia.

Dickie taking his nieces for a ride in a pedal car.

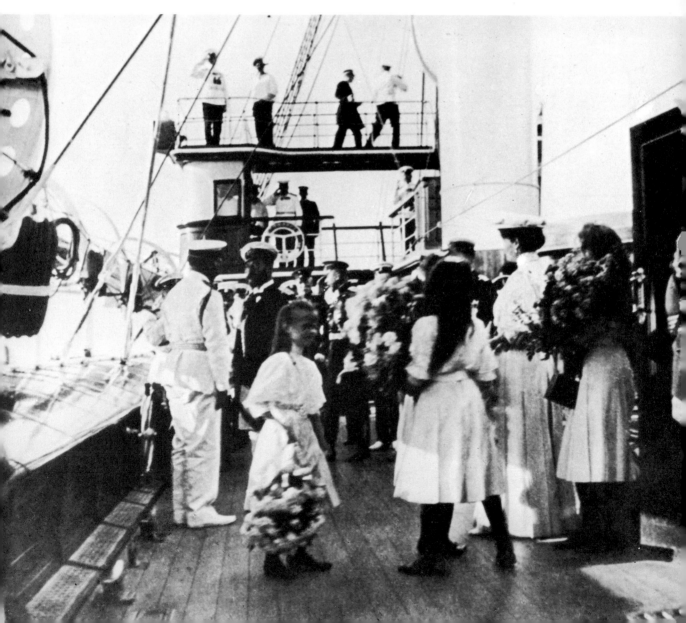

Far left
Dickie paddling on the beach at Hemmelmark with Helmine von Oertzen (Lady-in-Waiting), Louise and his Uncle Ernie. June 1909.

Left
The Russian Imperial yacht *Standardt* passed through the Kiel Canal on its way to England. On the breakwater are (left to right): Olga, Tatiana, Dickie, Anastasia and standing below them Marie and Uncle Ernie. 1909.

Right
On board *Standardt*. Left to right: Dickie, the Grand Duke of Hesse (Uncle Ernie), Tsar Nicholas II, Olga, Marie, Prince Sigismund.

Left to right: the Tsar, the Grand Duke of Hesse, Prince Sigismund (Cousin Bobby), Prince Waldemar of Prussia (Cousin Toddy), Dickie (seated). 'Bobby' (1896–1978) and 'Toddy' (1889–1945) were sons of Princess Henry of Prussia. Note the cavalry escort on the bank of the canal behind them.

Left
A meeting of Emperors on board *Standardt*. Left to right: Kaiser Wilhelm II, Tsar Nicholas II, Anastasia, Marie, the Tsarina and Olga

Overleaf
A selection of postcards sent at Christmas and Easter by the Russian Imperial Family. The shaky signature on the card dated 1910 'For dear Dicky' is that of Alexei, the six-year-old Tsarevitch. The last card is from Aunt Alix, the Tsarina. The pictures on the reverse of the postcards are illustrated in colour on page 20.

On 6 May 1910 King Edward VII died and he was deeply mourned by all those who had known and loved him. Prince Louis personally felt it very much for, ever since he had been a cadet in the *Ariadne* in 1869, Uncle Bertie had been the kindest of friends to him. As personal ADC to the Sovereign, Prince Louis escorted on foot the gun carriage bearing the coffin all through London, whilst the rest of his family, including Dickie, went to the actual funeral at Windsor.

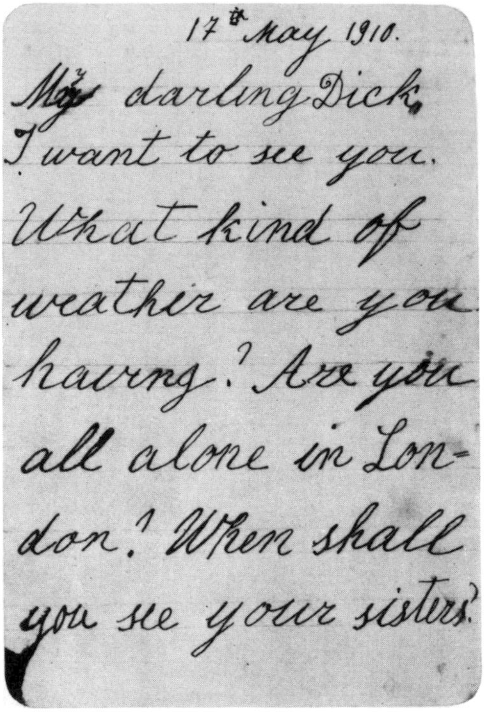

17th May 1910.

My darling Dick,
I want to see you.
What kind of weather are you having? Are you all alone in London? When shall you see your sisters?

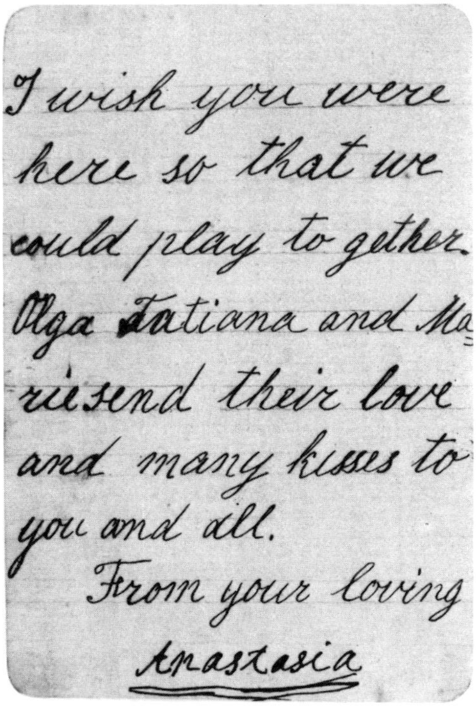

I wish you were here so that we could play to gether. Olga Tatiana and Marie send their love and many kisses to you and all.
From your loving
Anastasia

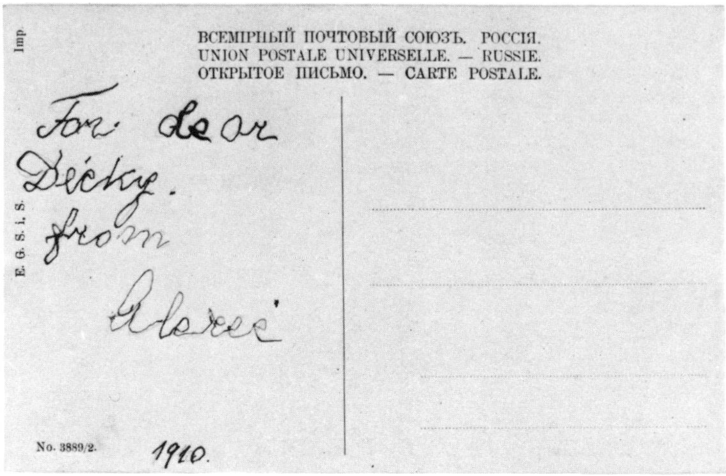

Imp

ВСЕМІРНЫЙ ПОЧТОВЫЙ СОЮЗЪ. РОССІЯ.
UNION POSTALE UNIVERSELLE. — RUSSIE.
ОТКРЫТОЕ ПИСЬМО. — CARTE POSTALE.

E. G. S. i. S.

For dear Dicky. from Alexei

No. 3889/2. 1910.

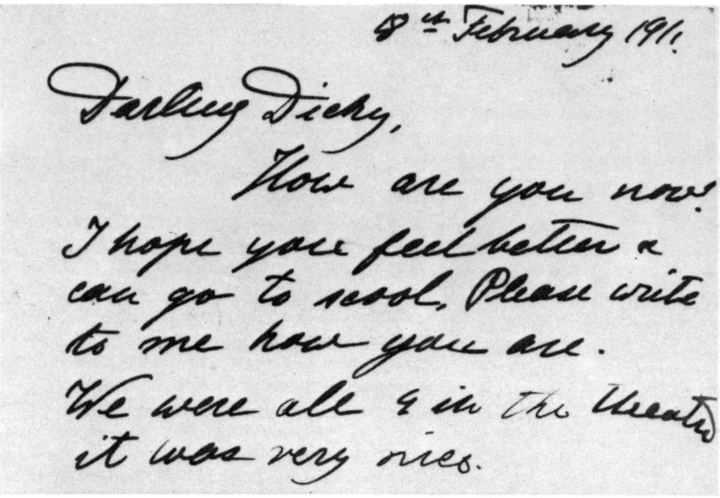

8th February 1911.

Darling Dicky,
How are you now?
I hope you feel better & can go to scool. Please write to me how you are.
We were all 4 in the theatre it was very nice.

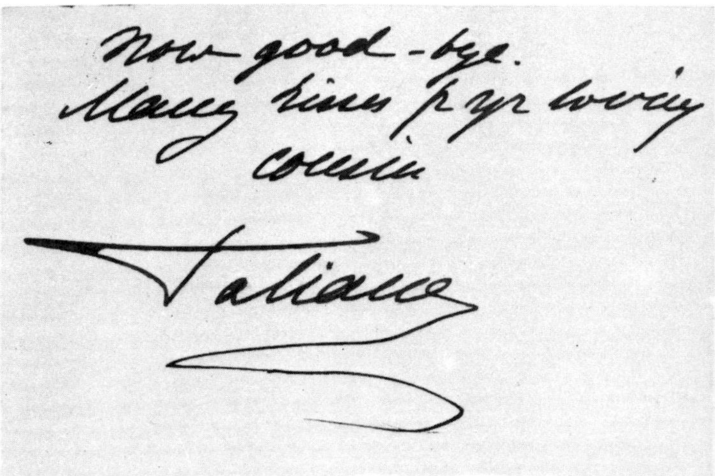

Now good-bye.
Many kisses fr yr loving cousin
Tatiana

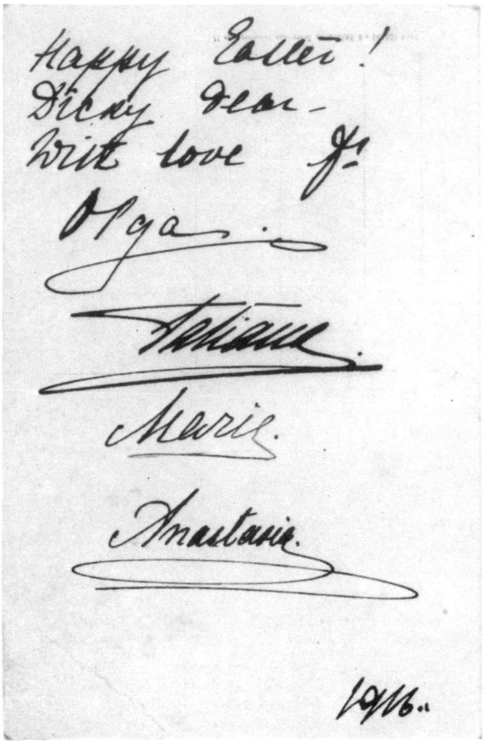

Happy Easter !
Dicky dear-
With love fr.
Olga.

Tatiana.

Marie.

Anastasia.

1916.

ПОЧТОВАЯ КАРТОЧКА.

Для письма.   Для адреса.

Happy Xmas
dear Dick
fr. Olga. —

Tatiana.

Marie.

Anastasia

1915.

Оберъ-офицеръ 11-го гусарскаго Изюмскаго
генерала Дорохова

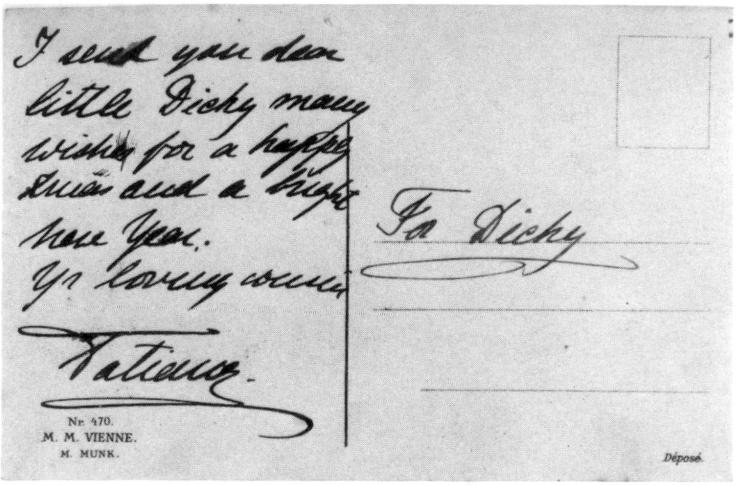

I send you dear
little Dicky many
wishes for a happy
Xmas and a happy
New Year.
Yr loving cousin

Tatiana.

Fa Dicky

Nr. 470.
M. M. VIENNE.
M. MUNK.

Déposé.

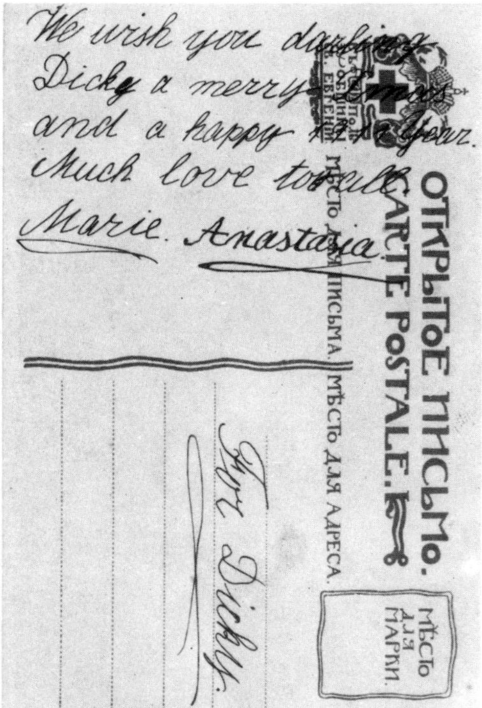

We wish you darling
Dicky a merry
and a happy New Year.
Much love to all
Marie. Anastasia

ОТКРЫТОЕ ПИСЬМО.
CARTE POSTALE.
мѣсто для письма. || мѣсто для адреса.

мѣсто
для
марки.

Fr. Dicky.

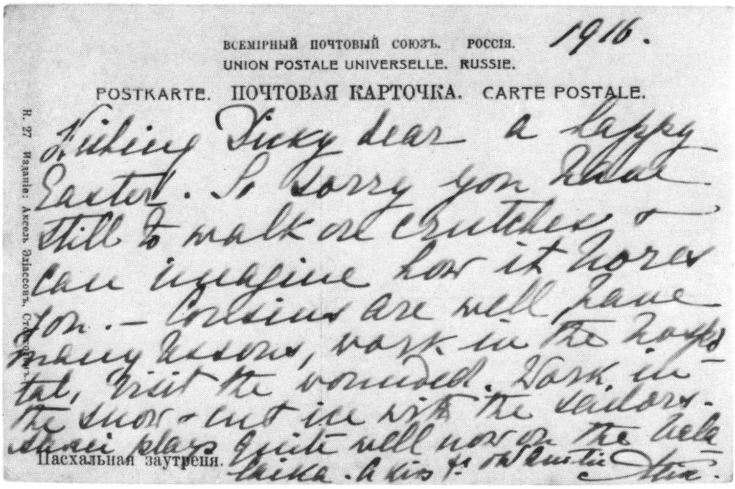

ВСЕМІРНЫЙ ПОЧТОВЫЙ СОЮЗЪ. РОССІЯ.
UNION POSTALE UNIVERSELLE. RUSSIE.
POSTKARTE. ПОЧТОВАЯ КАРТОЧКА. CARTE POSTALE.

1916.

Wishing Dicky dear a happy
Easter. So sorry you had
still to walk on crutches &
can imagine how it bores
you. — Cousins are well have
many lessons, work in the hospital, visit the wounded. Work in
the snow - cut ice with the sailors
three days. Quite well now on the whole.
Laika. A kiss fr Valentin. Anastasia

Пасхальная заутреня.

R. 27 Изданіе: Аксель Эляссонъ, Стокгольмъ.

Schloss Friedberg in Hesse, 1910. Left to right: Anastasia, Dolla, Alexei holding Louis, Prince of Hesse and the Rhine (Lu), Margarita, Olga, George Donatus, Hereditary Grand Duke of Hesse and the Rhine (Don) and Dickie.

Don, Dolla, Lu, Dickie, Margarita, Alexei with their nurses, Friedberg, 1910.

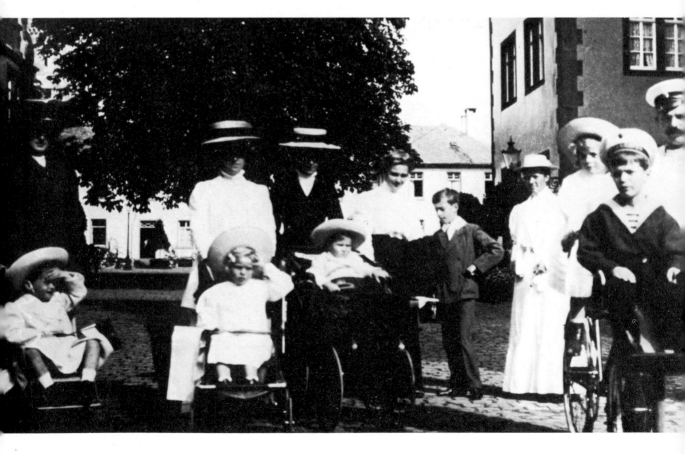

For the summer of 1910 the family rented a comfortable old-fashioned house with extensive pleasure grounds called Germains, near Chesham in Buckinghamshire, and at the beginning of May Princess Alice and her husband, Prince Andrew of Greece, came with their two little girls, Margarita and Dolla, to stay with them. Later that summer the family went first to Heiligenberg and then to Schloss Friedberg where there was a large family gathering as the Tsar, Tsarina and their five children had also come to stay with Grand Duke Ernest-Louis.

So far Dickie's experience of school had been confined to Macpherson's Gymnastic School in Sloane Street which he had entered in January 1905. This was run by a retired non-commissioned officer of the Blues (the Royal Horse Guards) who had the popular idea of having all drill exercises accompanied by the piano. In November 1909, with the family in residence at 35 Ennismore Gardens, Dickie began regularly to attend Mr Gladstone's day school for small boys at 35 Cliveden Place, Eaton Square.

Schloss Heiligenberg, 1910.
Dickie in his first Eton jacket.

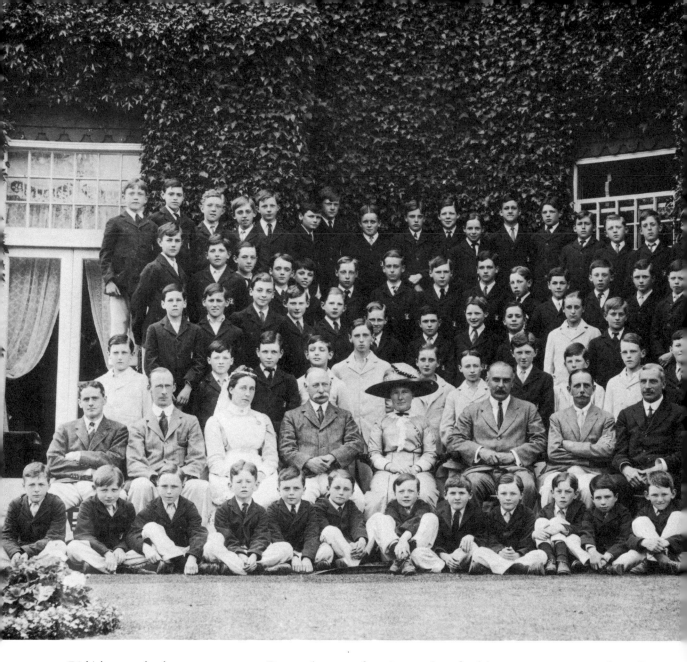

Dickie's prep-school was Locker's Park near Hemel Hempstead and this is the summer term 1911. Dickie is in the second row, seventh from the left. (The new comprehensive school at Hemel Hempstead is called Mountbatten School.)

But at the age of ten it was time for him to go to a proper boarding school, Locker's Park near Hemel Hempstead in Hertfordshire. The school was well run by Percy Christopherson and his wife. Dickie's mother continued to support him with letters full of restrained affection and good advice. Soon after he went there she wrote to him: 'I am proud to know you have made such a good beginning by your conduct and diligence, for I know it was not always easy for you. Nothing makes Papa and me so happy as to see that our children are doing their best at work & are honest & brave. Cleverness is not the chief thing, it is the willingness to do right & the effort made for it that really counts.'

40

At Locker's Park Dickie won himself a reputation and a bloody nose in the boxing ring, reaching the finals in the school tournament.

In February 1911 Dickie was struck down by an inflammation of the lungs. His mother visited him whenever she could and brought him, among other things, a new E. Nesbit book and a model destroyer to cheer him up. His brother Georgie managed to get leave and came to see him too. He talked enthusiastically of his life at sea, confirming Dickie in his determination to join the Navy as soon as possible.

In March Prince Louis took over command of the 3rd and 4th Divisions of the Home Fleet, which consisted of battleships, and in May the family moved to Admiralty House at Sheerness where Dickie joined them for his summer holidays.

That summer the family had its first experience of flying in an aeroplane. A group of young volunteer naval officers, supported by a most enthusiastic Prince Louis, who fought their battles with a very unsympathetic Admiralty, had formed the beginnings of naval aviation by being allowed to go to the airfield at Eastchurch on the Isle of Sheppey where the Short brothers had their works and tested out their aircraft. The senior officer was Lt Sampson who afterwards became an Air Commodore and greatly distinguished himself in the First World War. He had with him Lt Arthur Longmore, who later became Air Chief Marshal Sir Arthur Longmore, Air Commander Middle East during the first two years of the Second World War.

Prince Louis was taken up for a flight by Sampson who then took up Princess Louis. They had with them two of their children, Louise and Dickie, and Lt Longmore offered to take them up. He first took up Louise and then Dickie. In the S 27, the passenger had to sit on the petrol tank just behind and rather above the pilot, holding on to two struts, with his legs each side of the pilot's shoulders. There was quite a bumpy run before the plane took off and, when it did, the passenger was sitting absolutely exposed to the wind.

In October 1911 Winston Churchill went to the Admiralty as First Lord. Two months later Prince Louis returned to the Admiralty as Second Sea Lord and in that position initiated many of the overdue reforms which were carried out during Churchill's period of office. It was at this time that young Dickie first came to know Winston Churchill. He would sometimes walk home with Prince Louis after a day's work and call in at the family home.

In December 1912 Churchill appointed Prince Louis First Sea Lord and together they started a Naval War Staff. They revised the war plans, this time taking the Army into account and they decided on the strategy of distant blockade which was adopted from the moment war was declared. Dickie was entering the Navy at a historic moment.

A Naval Education

Dickie in the round jacket of a naval cadet proudly stands outside the First Sea Lord's residence, Mall House in Admiralty Arch. May 1913.

Right
Mr A. P. Boissier's Tutor set, June 1913. Dickie is seated on the grass third from the left.

O N 8 May 1913, barely six weeks before his thirteenth birthday, Dickie entered the Royal Naval College, Osborne as a naval cadet. In July he was laid up with scarlet fever and mumps. When he recovered he went with the family to Wolfsgarten where they were all taken for an afternoon tour in a large Zeppelin airship which flew all over the Grand Duchy of Hesse and circled Heiligenberg. This great dirigible was so carefully balanced that on landing each passenger had to be replaced by another person.

Life had been relatively easy at Locker's Park, but at Osborne things were harder: as a cousin of the King, of German descent, whose father was First Sea Lord, Dickie was subjected to some merciless ragging and bullying – the more so as, at first appearance, he seemed tender and unlikely to hit back. But he took it quite cheerfully and proved well able to defend himself.

It was at Osborne that Dickie first showed his prowess as an oarsman when he stroked the winning boat in the First Year Skiffs. This success was later repeated at the Royal Naval College, Dartmouth. Indeed he can proudly claim that he never lost any boat race in which he took part before the outbreak of war in 1939.

Churchill came down to Osborne to inspect the cadets and later, at supper, noticed Dickie and asked him if there were any complaints. Mountbatten remembers: 'Rather boldly, I said yes, there was something: we would like three sardines each for our Sunday supper, instead of two. This he promised to do, but the third sardine never materialized, so I felt rather let down.'

In May 1914, his second year at Osborne, Dickie developed whooping cough and had bronchitis on top of it. As soon as he was well enough he was sent for a change of air to a cottage at West Bay, near Bridport and Mr Lawrence Long, a former master at Gladstone's School, went with him as tutor.

In July a full test mobilization of the whole Fleet, including Reserves, was held instead of the usual manoeuvres. Prince Louis had been pressing for this for ten years but only succeeded in his time as Second Sea Lord, when he was the chief of all naval personnel. The machinery for getting the enlarged Navy out quickly in time of war had been worked out to the last detail, but it was essential to see whether it worked. It went off without a hitch. Churchill and Prince Louis personally inspected the process at Chatham, and officers were specially detached from the Admiralty to monitor progress at every port so that any shortcomings could be put right. To Dickie's great excitement the Osborne cadets were also mobilized and he was sent to his brother's ship, the *New Zealand*, where he was issued with a hammock and told where to sling it in a passageway. Georgie showed him round, and they had a grandstand view of the Royal Review which followed the mobilization. The whole Fleet – 59 battleships, 55 cruisers, 78 destroyers, 16 submarines and a host of lesser craft – was assembled at Spithead before King George V, who reviewed the forty miles of ships

Recovering from whooping cough and bronchitis at West Bay, near Bridport. The spaniel was called Aera.

Dickie in the uniform of a naval cadet, with his mother.

from the Royal Yacht, *Victoria and Albert*. Mountbatten remembers the spectacle as a 'sort of grand climax of two hundred years of British naval supremacy'. Churchill himself described the scene: 'It took more than six hours for this armada, every ship decked with flags and crowded with blue-jackets and marines, to pass with bands playing and at 15 knots before the Royal Yacht, while overhead the naval seaplanes and aeroplanes circled continuously.'

On 26 July 1914 Prince Louis took the most important decision of his life. It was a Sunday and the First Lord, the Prime Minister and most of the Cabinet were away for the weekend. The following day the men who had been called up for the test mobilization were due to be paid off and the Fleet would be dispersed. The international situation was worsening and it seemed madness to pass from a position of full naval preparedness into a state of weakness. Yet not to demobilize would be seen by some foreign powers as an act of war. It was a fearful decision to have to make but Prince Louis, on the basis of the information coming in to him, decided not to demobilize. He wrote out the telegrams ordering the Fleet to stand fast and Churchill, when he heard what Prince Louis had determined, gave his immediate approval. Thus, when on 4 August 1914 Britain went to war, Prince Louis could tell the King: 'We have the drawn sword in our hand.'

In that July of 1914 Princess Louis and her daughter Louise were in Russia aboard the Emperor's yacht on the Volga. Prince Louis and his son were to have joined them, but now instead Prince Louis had to telegraph St Petersburg asking that they should have a safe conduct home through Scandinavia. His son, Georgie, was in the Grand Fleet, and his nephew, Prince Maurice of Battenberg, in France in the 60th Rifles; but he also had relatives in the German Army and Navy, and the thought of the approaching war pained him deeply. He was comforted a little by the presence of his younger son, for the Osborne cadets were too young to fight, so Dickie came up to London to join his father at Mall House, the official residence of the First Sea Lord.

Mountbatten remembers his joy at being alone with his father at Mall House; Prince Louis always talked to his children as if they were grown up, and he confided in Dickie the inside story of the progression towards war, and finally – as all hope of peace died – the strategies to be employed at the onset of war and the possible actions of the enemy. Both the sixty-year-old Admiral and the fourteen-year-old cadet wore their uniforms with the stylish care the father had passed on to the son. When Victoria and Louise arrived in England on 16 August, after a difficult and dangerous journey through Sweden, Victoria found her husband 'absorbed in his work which went on at night as well as by day', and her son 'finding occupation in the care of some white mice'.

The war that followed was, to begin with, strangely unspectacular for the Navy. They were ready for battle, and they, and the British public, expected straightforward sea victories in the tradition of Nelson. But the German Fleet stayed in port, and British trading vessels were able to continue serving the island's material needs without interruption. There were some sea battles but the man in the street was not impressed by the Navy's achievements.

In the first months of the war a state of hysteria gripped the country. Invasion scares were numerous. Anti-German feeling came to a head in attacks on Germans and Austrians living in Britain; German churches were stoned, German shops looted. Mountbatten remembers that people 'insulted German governesses; they wouldn't listen to German music; they would even kick dachshunds in the street; they saw spies under every bed'.

Feeling against Prince Louis spread to the popular newspapers, and even to a small part of the Navy itself. Soon his old enemies, including those who had been affronted by his reforms in the Navy, were calling for his resignation. His German connections, many people realized, could be useful; his knowledge of the German character and methods might help in the war but he had had a castle in Germany, his family had often visited the country, and detractors claimed that his knowledge of British ways might be proving equally useful to the

Germans. Among those who knew him well, his loyalty to the country he had served for forty-six years was not in question, but the outcry against him grew to such proportions that Prince Louis sent in his resignation, and it was accepted. Churchill did his best to soften the blow by publicly paying tribute to Prince Louis' work, and acknowledged that 'the first step which secured the timely concentration of the Fleet was taken by you'. But the public humiliation hit Prince Louis very hard, and it had its effect on his son. Dickie would probably have had a meteoric career in the Navy anyway, but the burning sense of injustice spurred him on to even greater heights, until eventually he held the same office – First Sea Lord – as that from which his father resigned and, almost incredibly, they were both appointed by the same man, Winston Churchill.

Late in 1914 Dickie passed out of Osborne and went to Royal Naval College, Dartmouth. Here he really came into his own and excelled at many sports and among other things was placed second in fencing with the single stick – a rough unpopular sport.

Late in 1914 Dickie passed out of Osborne and went on to Royal Naval College, Dartmouth.

Driving the family's Wolseley Stellite car in the drive of Kent House, Isle of Wight, 1916.

Mountbatten before joining HMS *Lion*, Beatty's flagship, July 1916.

He broke his leg just before his final examinations, and had to take them in hospital. He was upset at only coming eighteenth out of a class of eighty but in the final intensive three-months' course at Keyham he came top.

His parents had in November 1914 retired to Kent House in the Isle of Wight which Princess Louis had inherited from her aunt, Princess Louise, Duchess of Argyll, and it was there the young cadet spent his leaves.

He was too late to fight in the Battle of Jutland, that curious battle in which the British Navy faced the might of the German Navy and was not destroyed, thus in a sense gaining a victory, although its losses were heavy. Georgie had taken part in the battle, and Dickie cursed his bad luck at missing it, and at joining the *Lion*, the flagship of Vice-Admiral Sir David Beatty, just seven weeks too late, when she had come back to Rosyth for repair. Beatty was his hero but life for a young midshipman in the *Lion* was hard, even if glorious. Mountbatten remembers that 'in some respects conditions were not very different from those in Nelson's days. The midshipmen slept in hammocks, which we hung wherever we could find a space – we had no proper quarters of our own. I had to sling my hammock under a police-light, which was never switched off: it was just a few inches above my face. I got used to sleeping with a handkerchief over my eyes.' The midshipmen, or 'snotties' as they were called, were beaten for the most trifling failures but this bullying tradition was dying out, and eventually Admiral Beatty stepped in to end it.

The work was hard too. The ship ran on coal, and to 'coal ship' after an expedition took ten to twelve hours and involved the whole ship's company. 'One becomes absolutely encrusted in dust from head to foot. The junior snotties only had small tin baths to wash it all off in afterwards; it hung about one for days.' But morale was high; the battle-cruisers were proud of their efficient coaling, which enabled them to take on board 250–300 tons an hour, but several times the *Lion* took in over 400 tons an hour. Early in 1917 Dickie was transferred to Beatty's new flagship, *Queen Elizabeth*. Beatty was now Commander-in-Chief of the Grand Fleet.

In 1917 the Battenbergs lost their name and their German titles. The anti-German hysteria was reaching new heights, and the government decided that they had to advise King George V that members of the Royal Family should take British names. The King's family took the name of Windsor; Queen Mary's family changed theirs from Teck to Cambridge, and Prince Louis changed his family name from Battenberg to Mountbatten and the King bestowed on him the titles of Marquess of Milford Haven, Earl of Medina and Viscount Alderney. He became known by the first; his eldest son, Georgie, assumed his father's second title of Earl of Medina and Dickie became Lord Louis Mountbatten.

Midshipman aboard *Queen Elizabeth*, Beatty's new flagship.

Admiral Wemyss and Admiral Beatty (Commander-in-Chief Grand Fleet) on board *Queen Elizabeth*, 1918.

Above and far right
The autumn of 1918, father and
sons now renamed the Marquess
of Milford Haven (Prince Louis),
Earl of Medina (Georgie) and
Lord Louis Mountbatten.

All during 1917 and the first months of 1918 the family, especially
Princess Louis, made desperate efforts to keep in touch with their
imperial relatives in Russia. The Royal Families of Europe were being
forced from their thrones into abdication, exile or even worse. Anti-
Tsarist feeling in Russia had been increasing. In 1917 the first Russian
Revolution took place, the Tsar abdicated and he and his family were
held at Tsarskoe Selo. This was sad news, but there was still hope that
they might escape alive. In October of that year the Bolshevik
Revolution dashed the hopes of their relatives in England even further.
They feared the worst, but it was not until 2 September 1918 that they
were officially told that the whole family had been assassinated. They
were all shot together; the young Tsarevitch, who was just fourteen
years old, did not die at once and was shot three more times. Anastasia,
the youngest of the girls, was bayoneted eighteen times.

Through the anguish of the loss of her sister, brother-in-law,
nephew and four nieces, Princess Louis grasped the hope that her sister
Ella, the Grand Duchess Serge of Russia, might still be alive. But in
November she heard that as far back as July the saintly Ella had been
thrown down a mineshaft with several others. Bombs were thrown
after them, but not all were killed immediately. When the bodies were
recovered, some had their wounds dressed with strips torn from the
Martha and Mary habit which Ella always wore. Only Ella could have
done this, and she must have needed all her faith and courage.

In July 1918 Mountbatten, on promotion to Sub-Lieutenant, had a
break from the routine of service on ship and at base, as he was one of
the junior officers allowed to visit the Western Front. They were
shown the administrative machinery running a major land war, but the
abiding impression was the horror of the Front. Mountbatten
remembers: 'A Second-Lieutenant in the Army, I discovered, had an
expectation of life of only about six or seven weeks on the Western
Front, which was a shocking thought. On the other hand, when
disaster occurred at sea, it was usually pretty complete disaster . . . I
myself saw the battleship *Vanguard* blow up at anchor in Scapa Flow,
and took a boat away to look for survivors – there were only two.' The
conditions in which so many men were fighting and dying had a strong
impact on him, which he was to remember when he came to
Combined Operations Headquarters in the Second World War and
even more so when he became Supreme Allied Commander, South
East Asia.

In November 1918 the war ended. Mountbatten was eighteen; he
had spent the last five years training and at war, and laid the foundation
of his naval career; now it was time for a change of scene, and a little
relaxation.

Friend to the Prince of Wales

WHEN the war ended, Mountbatten was a Sub-Lieutenant, Second-in-Command of an anti-submarine vessel with a crew of fifty, the *P31* in the Portsmouth Escort Flotilla. During the war Mountbatten obtained special permission to embark his father aboard *P31* on a routine escort trip to Le Havre and back. This was a great joy to both of them.

Mountbatten's pay was five shillings a day and he got an allowance from his father of £300 a year, so he could afford to run a small car. For the first time in his life he had time for parties, dances and pretty girls.

He was a popular First Lieutenant and kept the *P31* happy and efficient. *P31* later took part in the Baltic operations, but without Mountbatten, for in the autumn of 1919 he went to Cambridge for two terms, as part of the Admiralty's policy of providing some general education for the 'war babies' who had gone to sea at a very early age. He went to Christ's, read Ethnology and the History of Geographical Discoveries as voluntary subjects, and played a prominent part in the Union, where in his second term he led the debate against Oxford on the motion: 'The time is ripe for a Labour government.' As leader, he could invite an outside guest, so he telephoned Winston Churchill, now back in power as Secretary of State for War, and he came down to help oppose the motion. Needless to say, Oxford was overwhelmingly defeated!

This was a new world for him and he made many new friends. Cambridge was followed by an equally eye-opening experience for a young man. He had always been a good friend of his cousin Edward, the Prince of Wales, known in the family as David, and in 1920 he was invited to accompany the Prince as Flag-Lieutenant to his Chief of Staff, Rear-Admiral Sir Lionel Halsey, on a tour of New Zealand, Australia and the West Indies in the battle-cruiser *Renown*. One purpose of the tour was to improve relations with parts of the British Empire, and Mountbatten looked forward with interest to seeing all the distant territories he had helped to defend. There was no air travel at that time and most of the Empire was difficult to reach.

Mountbatten kept a diary throughout the tour, and got to know his cousin even better than before, realizing that under the charming and vivacious exterior he was an introspective person, liable to periods of deep depression. They had always been friends, for the Prince had had a naval career a few years in advance of his own, and Mountbatten's role

Previous page
The *P31* had a ship's company of
fifty and they were very proud
of her. Mountbatten is sixth
from the left in the second row.

Right
Mountbatten's father and
mother looked over the ship in
1919 when *P31* took part in the
Thames River Pageant.

Left
First Lieutenant and earning five
shillings a day.

'War babies' were sent to complete their education interrupted by the war. Geoffrey Shakespeare was President of the Cambridge Union in February 1920 when this picture was taken. Mountbatten is in naval officer's uniform.

had even then at times been that of cheering up his cousin, who when he was depressed often expressed the wish that he could change places with the ebullient Mountbatten. The responsibilities of being Prince of Wales sometimes weighed heavily on him, though he worked very hard and always kept up a genial appearance through his many official duties.

Not the least disturbing of his experiences on tour must have been the traditional ceremony that took place at the crossing of the Equator on 17 April 1920. Mountbatten described it in his diary: 'At two bells in the forenoon watch a fanfare of trumpets announced the arrival of King Neptune. The Chief Herald came on to the quarterdeck leading the procession. Next came the Chief Bears, after these followed the Judge, two of his Majesty's Bodyguard, and his Aquatic Majesty King Neptune himself, accompanied by his Queen Amphitrite and his Secretary. The Doctor, the three Barbers and four more of the Bodyguard were followed by the rest of the Bears, the Deep Sea Police, the Barbers' Assistants and the Doctors' Assistants . . . HRH sat down in the Barbers' chair, and the Doctor took his temperature, proclaiming it to be normal . . . His Majesty, however, objected to this, pointing to

Outside the Flag-Lieutenant's cabin, Sir Godfrey Thomas and Mountbatten.

At sea in the battle-cruiser *Renown*. Left to right on pogo sticks: Dudley North, Mountbatten (actually in the air) and Sir Godfrey Thomas, the Prince of Wales' Private Secretary.

Mountbatten, Flag-Lieutenant to Rear-Admiral Sir Lionel Halsey, accompanied the Prince of Wales on a Tour of New Zealand, Australia and the West Indies, 1920.

Fishing in the Chagres River,
Panama.

Crossing the Line ceremony.

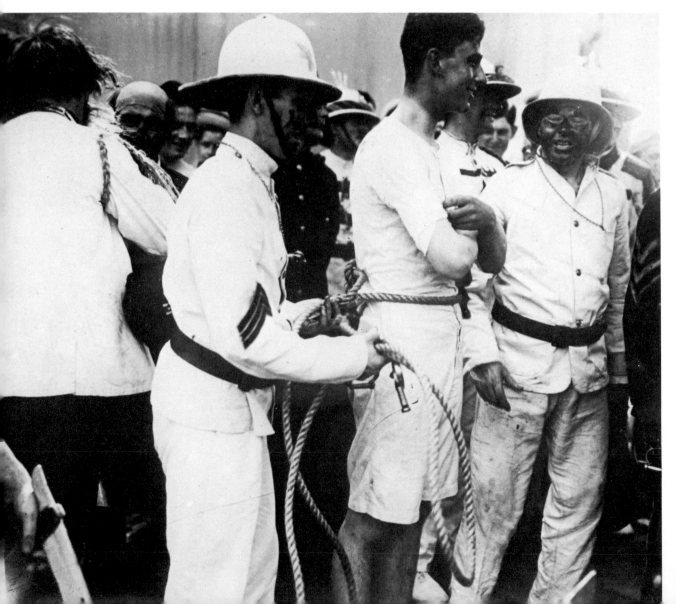

Canvas bath on deck, the Prince of Wales and Mountbatten.

Renown at Panama – a fishing party for tarpon. Left to right: Mountbatten, the Prince of Wales, Lt Billyarde-Leake (who was the youngest DSO at Zeebrugge in 1918), and Lieutenant Commander Lyster (who was to command the air strike at Taranto in 1940 which crippled the Italian Fleet).

Sydney, July 1920. Left to right: Ursula Catteral (whom Mountbatten did not meet again for another fifty-five years), Mountbatten, Mollie Little and the Prince of Wales.

HRH's shaking knees. The Doctor . . . gave HRH a No. 9 pill (which was about the size of a golf ball). The Chief Barber then lathered him thoroughly and shaved him with a razor whose blade was three feet long. Suddenly the chair tilted backwards, and before he knew where he was, HRH was in the grip of the Bears, who ducked him along the entire length of the bath.' Mountbatten himself had an even worse ducking.

Both New Zealand and Australia welcomed the Prince with great demonstrations of affection. Thousands of people came to meet him and shake his hand wherever he went, including many returned servicemen of the Anzacs – the Australian and New Zealand Army Corps. The Prince's right hand took such a crushing on these occasions that he had to resort to shaking hands with his left hand.

The Prince and Mountbatten spent three months in Australia, visiting every state and capital and also parts of the outback. On 5 July

1920 the Prince and his party were on their way by train from Manjimupp to Bridgetown in Western Australia. It had poured with rain most of the previous night and it was still pelting. The Royal coach was at the end of the train. The next coach ahead was the Ministerial coach and just in front of this ran No. 1 sleeping car which accommodated the staff. Then came a dining car and four more coaches, the whole being drawn by two very heavy and powerful locomotives. A short distance ahead of this train ran the pilot train and at frequent intervals along the line 'line watchers' were stationed to report if anything went wrong.

At 2.45 p.m. a series of violent jolts was felt by the occupants of the last three coaches. The Prince of Wales and Admiral Halsey who were in the end compartment guessed that their coach must be off the line. Mountbatten, who was in No. 1 coach when he first noticed the jolting, dashed back to the Ministerial coach. He at once looked round for the communication cord, but found none, as they were not fitted in Australian trains at that time. He then ran forward to get the engine stopped just as the last two coaches overturned with a great crash, dragging No. 1 coach off the rails and listing it over to the left. Luckily the train had not been travelling at its normal speed, as the line had been obstructed just previously by a cow, which the Prince of Wales later declared deserved the MVO.

Fortunately, the specially fitted strong couplings held, and the deadweight of the rear coaches brought the train to a standstill in a very short time. Mountbatten jumped out of No. 1 coach and raced back to the Royal coach which was lying on its side on a slightly sloping embankment with the wheels considerably higher than the roof. Water was pouring from the tanks on the roof and there was no sign of life until in answer to a hail a few choice but unrepeatable words from the Prince of Wales set everyone's mind at rest. As the coaches overturned HRH had rolled himself up into a ball, putting his feet against the end of his bunk, so that eventually he found himself with his weight on his feet.

Faint cries of 'help' came from the drain pipe of the rear compartment of the Ministerial coach where the Minister of Woods and Forests had been caught literally with his trousers down. The officials responsible for the Prince of Wales' safety were still looking very white when HRH himself appeared through one of the corridor windows and cheerfully remarked: 'Well, anyway, at last we have done something which was not on the official programme.'

The Prince of Wales and party then examined the line, which was torn up and twisted for a distance of 80 yards behind the rear coach as though it had been shelled. For another 230 yards behind this again the marks on the sleepers indicated that the coaches had been off the rails for all this distance. There is no doubt that everyone had a most miraculous escape. Had the train been travelling faster or had the embankment been steeper the accident would almost certainly have proved fatal.

Overleaf: left
July 1920, near Manjimupp in Western Australia, the railway line gave way derailing the train. Mountbatten crawls out of the window of the Royal coach.

Overleaf: top right
The overturned coaches.

Overleaf: bottom right
Left to right: Chief Inspector Burt, Mountbatten and the Prince of Wales.

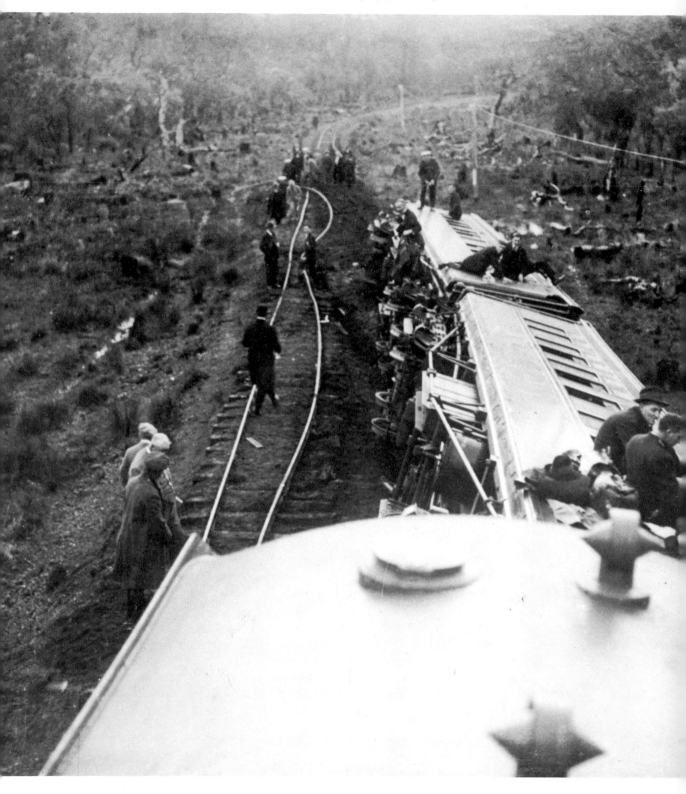

After Australia the *Renown* went on to Fiji, Samoa, Honolulu, and then to Colon via the Panama Canal. In Honolulu they had a week's holiday in the Moana Hotel and enjoyed surf riding off Waikiki beach. Each had an expert Kanaka surf rider to help. The Prince had David Kahanamoku and Mountbatten had Kalakaua Kawananakoa. There then followed a series of visits to British Guyana and islands in the West Indies and finally a visit to Bermuda, and the party returned to Portsmouth on 11 October 1920.

In 1921 Mountbatten found himself in charge of a platoon of fifty-six naval ratings during the State of Emergency caused by the miners' strike. Privately he expressed the hope that he and his men would not be used against the strikers – as he put it, 'unfortunate people who were trying to obtain better conditions'. They were not used, and he was able to return to his ship, at that time the *Repulse*, sister ship of the *Renown*. They were due to go up to Invergordon and his father came on board at Sheerness and sailed up with them. His father had been promoted to Admiral of the Fleet on 4 August 1921, the seventh anniversary of the outbreak of war, in recognition of his services to the Royal Navy which he had joined fifty-three years before and as a partial atonement for the injustice that had forced him to retire from the post of First Sea Lord in October 1914.

Honolulu, September 1920, Mountbatten at the end of a surfboard run.

Waikiki, Honolulu, 1 September 1920. Left to right: Prince Kalakaua Kawananakoa, Mountbatten, the Prince of Wales and D. P. Kahanamoku.

Waiting for surfboards.

Mrs Rhodes, a friend, exchanges headgear with Mountbatten.

Trinidad, September 1920, the Prince of Wales and Mountbatten.

Watching a polo match.

His father clearly enjoyed the impromptu cruise. It was nearly ten years since he had set foot in a Dreadnought and the ward-room gave him an affectionate welcome. He caught a chill and had a touch of lumbago but seemed to recover. On his return to London he planned to go out to Constantinople to join Georgie on board the cruiser *Cardiff*, but this was not to be. On 11 September he met his wife and his daughter Louise at his club in Piccadilly and they talked of family affairs. He complained of not feeling well and went to bed. The doctor came and Princess Louis went out to buy the medicine prescribed for him. When she came back he was dead.

66

© 1920

Preserving law and order during the Coal Strike, 1921.

Cowes, August 1921, Mountbatten was a guest of Cornelius Vanderbilt, on board his yacht. Left to right: Grace Vanderbilt, Colin Davidson, Dick Curzon and Mountbatten playing a 'Swanee whistle'.

Larking about.

Mountbatten and Dick Curzon
'chumming up'.

Above: right
Mountbatten, Dick Curzon,
Grace Vanderbilt and Colin
Davidson.

Below
Mountbatten and Edwina
Ashley at Georgie and his wife
Nada's house at Southsea.

When his father had left him at Invergordon, Mountbatten had gone on leave to Dunrobin Castle nearby to stay the weekend with the Duke and Duchess of Sutherland and a large house-party. One of the guests was Edwina Ashley, a beautiful, intelligent girl whom Mountbatten had already met and to whom he found himself strongly attracted. The arrival of a telegram with the sad news of his father's unexpected death shattered the weekend and prevented, at least for the moment, any further thoughts of love. It was a terrible blow to Mountbatten who adored his father, and he hurried home for the funeral.

Another of the guests at Dunrobin was the Prince of Wales who shared Mountbatten's grief and sense of loss. He knew it was essential that the young man should not have time to dwell on the tragic event and this strengthened his resolve to take him on the second Empire Tour which was shortly to begin. The 1921–2 Tour took the Prince and Mountbatten to India, Burma, Ceylon, Malaya, and Japan and proved to be for the most part a tremendous success. Everywhere huge crowds came out to see the Prince and, with Mountbatten, he had the opportunity of getting to know the rulers and statesmen who were to play an important part in changing the world.

This was Mountbatten's first visit to Japan, which he found exotic and fascinating, but it was his introduction to India which was to prove for him the most significant part of the Tour. India was still the 'brightest jewel' of the British Crown. The Royal party was entertained in great palaces to lavish spectacles and banquets, but the pomp and ceremony could not disguise the desperate poverty, the prevalence of disease and the regularly returning nightmare of famine.

70

Left
The Prince of Wales and Mountbatten on the Second Empire Tour visited Aden in November 1921. This enthusiastic reception was not 'official' and all the more welcome for that.

Right
The King's Messenger Race at the Malta Gymkhana. Mountbatten wheeling the Prince of Wales, Sir Godfrey Thomas looking on.

Below
The Prince of Wales' informality greatly pleased the crowds who came to see him on these Tours.

Mountbatten on his elephant after bagging his first tiger, Nepalese Terai, December 1921.

The Prince of Wales waits for the tiger in his howdah with Burt and his valet, Frederick Smith.

Mountbatten with a black buck he shot in Rajputana.

Gwalior; the children of Maharaja Scindia, George and Mary, named after the King and Queen, dressed up as Sepoys in the Gwalior army. George became a good friend of Mountbatten's.

Against this background, and despite Britain's contribution to modern India, there was a growing demand for independence. In addition, this was felt to be the promised reward for India's efforts during the First World War when over a million Indians had enlisted under the British Flag. Thus, when the Prince of Wales and Mountbatten arrived in Bombay, there were demonstrations and riots and Gandhi was demanding a peaceful boycott of the Tour. Although this was a failure, it proved a great strain on the Prince and the situation worsened when the Government imprisoned Gandhi. Mountbatten had attempted to meet Gandhi, and even have him introduced to the Prince, but the Government of India forbade it.

Mountbatten fell in love with India. First of all there was the sheer magnificence of the Maharajas and Nawabs ruling in great state, often with small armies and, in one case, even an air force to bolster their position. He made many personal friends among the Maharajas and their heirs and it was they who helped him to learn to play polo, a game which became quite a passion. He became one of Britain's best players, passing on his love for the game to his nephews and great-nephew, Prince Charles.

India, November 1921. A visit
to Maharaja (Gaekwar) of Baroda.
Arriving at Laxmi Vilas Palace.

January 1922, visiting Maharaja
Scindia of Gwalior.

The Honourable Edward
Pleydell-Bouverie and
Mountbatten at the Viceregal
Lodge in Old Delhi, February
1922. Pleydell-Bouverie was
Flag Lieutenant to Vice-Admiral
Clinton Baker, Commander-in-
Chief East Indies.

A relaxed Mountbatten at
Viceregal Lodge.

But there was another reason why India was particularly significant
for Mountbatten. He had been writing to Edwina Ashley all through
the Tour, describing his impressions and urging her to come out and
see him. Edwina devised a scheme whereby she could meet him briefly
on the Tour. Although she had inherited her grandfather's fortune she
could not have the benefit of it until she was twenty-one or married, so
she borrowed £100 to come out on a one-way ticket and stay with the
Viceroy, Lord Reading, in Delhi. On 14 February 1922 – St Valentine's
Day – there was a dance in the Viceregal Lodge and Mountbatten's
diary records: 'I danced 1 and 2 with Edwina. She had 3 and 4 with
David, and the fifth dance we sat out in her sitting-room, when I asked
her if she would marry me, and she said she would.'

In the television series he made about his life and times in 1967
Mountbatten said: 'In India I found three loves, though on three very
different planes. The first of them was India herself . . . Staying with the
Princes I found my second love: polo . . . And finally, my real love . . .'

'My Real Love'

EDWINA CYNTHIA ASHLEY was born on 28 November 1901 and was named after her godfather, King Edward VII. Her father, Colonel Wilfred Ashley (later Lord Mount Temple), was the grandson of the seventh Earl of Shaftesbury. His ancestors included the American Indian Princess, Pocahontas. He had a magnificent estate, Broadlands in Hampshire, which his great-grandmother, the Countess Cowper, had inherited from her second husband the famous 3rd Lord Palmerston. Edwina's mother, Maudie, was the daughter of the financier Sir Ernest Cassel. Maud Ashley died in 1911 when Edwina was just ten years old and from then on she, and her much younger sister Mary, spent a good deal of their time with their grandfather.

Edwina's father married again when she was fourteen and she was sent to school at Eastbourne and later to a domestic science school in Suffolk. From the time she left school life began to improve for her. Her grandfather arranged with her father that she should come to live with him and at the age of eighteen she took up her new role as hostess for him at his sumptuous mansion in London, Brook House, and made her triumphant debut in London Society where her success was phenomenal. But her life was not altogether an easy one, for as much as her grandfather adored her, he was an exacting person and expected her to devote a considerable part of her time to entertaining his elderly friends, who ranged from Kings and their entourages to city magnates and bankers from all over the world.

The Prince of Wales described his friend at the age of twenty-one as 'a vigorous and high spirited young man who became the instigator of many an unexpected diversion outside the official programme', and it was with this attractive, good-looking young man that Edwina had fallen in love. The announcement was made from the Viceregal Lodge on the night that the Prince's party left India. Mountbatten required Royal consent for the marriage, but the Prince of Wales was delighted with the match and quickly obtained the King's blessing. Lady Reading, the Vicereine, was not so sure, and wrote to Edwina's aunt: 'I am afraid she has definitely made up her mind about him. I hoped she would have cared for someone older, with more of a career before him.' Mountbatten's mother, Princess Louis (Victoria), also took Edwina to her heart. They were both highly intelligent women of strong personality and insatiable curiosity. They cared deeply about

Opposite page
Lady Mountbatten painted by
P. A. de Laszlo. 1924.

Overleaf
Lord and Lady Mountbatten
at Broadlands in 1959.

The day after the engagement
was announced, Mountbatten
and Edwina Ashley,
15 February 1922.

Edwina Ashley.

The Royal party travelled on to Japan in February 1922. The Prince of Wales in the uniform of Colonel of the Welsh Guards is met by the Emperor's son, Prince Hirohito (the present Emperor) who was then the Regent.

Carp fishing. In the background the Earl of Cromer, Chief of Staff to the Prince of Wales.

Prince Regent Hirohito, half hidden by Mountbatten, watches the Prince of Wales practising with a wooden sword-club.

Overleaf
This photograph of the Royal party dressed as Coolies taken at the end of the Japanese Tour scandalised the Imperial Court. Left to right: 'Fruity' Metcalfe, the Prince of Wales and Mountbatten.

Overleaf
The Prince of Wales, Bruce Ogilvy and Mountbatten stop to view Fujiyama.

people and could be considered lifelong liberal progressives. For Edwina, Victoria took the place in her affections of the mother she had lost so young.

Victoria was, however, worried about the disparity in fortune between Edwina, heir to a large fortune, and Mountbatten with only a very modest income. She felt he might be tempted to try less hard in his naval career or even leave the Navy altogether. In the event her worries were proved totally unfounded.

The visit to Japan was fascinating and an enormous success. It was certainly an eye-opener for Mountbatten who took note of her resources, her navy and army, and the growing militaristic nationalism. However, Mountbatten noted in his diary at the time that he feared the Japanese less now that he knew them to a certain extent, though he added that unrest was growing among the working classes and strikes and May Day disturbances had already started. He went on to say that their leaders thought that a war might save them as the people were still ultra-patriotic and added 'this is the war I fear'.

The Royal party finally arrived back at Plymouth on 21 June having covered a total of 40,600 miles during the Tour. Mountbatten was once more reunited with Edwina. The young couple were both keen to be married as early as possible and the wedding took place on 18 July 1922 at St Margaret's, Westminster. It was the social event of the season. A great gathering of Royalty was led by King George V and Queen Mary, and included the King's mother, Queen Alexandra, Tsar Alexander III's widow, the Dowager Tsarina (Aunt Minnie), and many Dukes and Duchesses, Princes and Princesses. The Prince of Wales was best man. Included among the seven bridesmaids were the bride's sister, Mary Ashley, her cousin, Joan Pakenham, Lady Mary Ashley-Cooper, and Mountbatten's four young Greek nieces, Princess Margarita, Princess Theodora, Princess Sophie and Princess Cecile of Greece (Prince Philip's sisters).

The bridegroom and best man arrive at St Margaret's, Westminster.

The King arrives.

The King greets his mother, Queen Alexandra.

Overleaf
The wedding group, 18 July 1922. Standing, left to right: Princess Margarita, Lord Mountbatten, Lady Mountbatten, the Prince of Wales, Princess Theodora. Sitting, left to right: Miss Mary Ashley, Miss Joan Pakenham, Princess Sophie, Lady Mary Ashley-Cooper, Princess Cecile.

Overleaf
The bride and bridegroom leaving the church.

According to *The Times* 'A discreet murmur of admiration rose from the congregation as the bride entered on the arm of her father . . . the bride's gown [was] conspicuous by its combination of simplicity and richness. Of dull silver tissue cut on long, straight lines, with a waistless bodice, mitten sleeves and round neck, its effect was of subdued splendour. Narrow stole panels, of unequal length, embroidered with crystal and diamanté, hung from either hip. The train, four yards in length, was of fifteenth-century point lace mounted on cloth of silver and edged with a heavier border of Spanish point lace, forming a stole drapery across the shoulders. The tissue foundation was turned back at the edge over the lace, so as to form, as it were, a frame for it.'

Left to right: Mountbatten's brother Georgie, Viscount Lascelles, the Prince of Wales, the Princess Royal, the Duke of York, Prince George (later Duke of Kent).

King George V, Queen Alexandra and Queen Mary leaving the church.

The two Queens talking to Princess Sophie of Greece, one of the bridesmaids, while the King greets Princess Theodora (Dolla).

The Prince of Wales leaving the church with the Princess Royal, Viscountess Lascelles. He wrote to Mountbatten: '. . . no-one could have had the wind up more than your best man!'

Queen Mary.

Sailors of HMS *Renown* pull the bridal car from St Margaret's.

Officers of the *Renown* formed a guard of honour, and a gun crew of sailors drew the bridal car away from the church to the glittering reception at Brook House. The honeymoon began at Broadlands, the home of Edwina's father, and 'a most convenient part of England for the naval world – 75 miles from London, 30 from Portsmouth, 40 from Weymouth and not too far from Plymouth', to quote Mountbatten. They had driven down in the bride's present to the groom, a Barker Cabriolet Rolls-Royce which Mountbatten, with his great love of cars, adored.

92

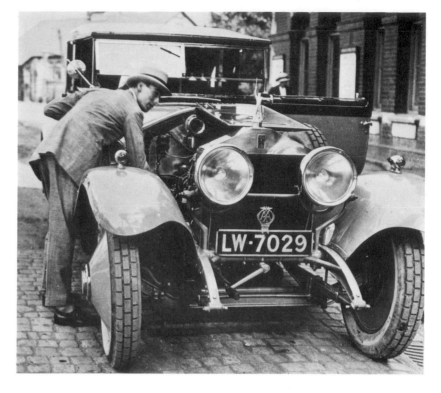

Mountbatten checking the engine of his 1919 Rolls-Royce, the bride's present to the bridegroom.

On honeymoon at Wolfsgarten, August 1922. Mountbatten is at the Opel racetrack at Rüsselsheim and the car is the new Opel Racer. Behind the car is young Prince Louis of Hesse.

Then with six months on half-pay Mountbatten and his bride began a trip through France and Spain to Santander to stay with his cousin Queen Ena and King Alfonso. Then across to Germany to stay with 'Uncle Ernie', the Grand Duke of Hesse, at Wolfsgarten, and then came the big excitement, a visit to America. The Mountbattens made a very favourable impact almost as soon as they arrived in Washington. They met President Harding and many other important people. Mountbatten made a major speech at a Navy League Dinner packed with Admirals and senior officers. This he remembers as being quite an ordeal for a young Lieutenant.

Mountbatten and Edwina during a trip in *Maid of the Mists* at the foot of Niagara Falls.

Fourth day out – after breakfast.

The Mountbatten party travelled in this private luxury car attached to the Transcontinental Topeka, Aitchison and Santa Fé train. Left to right: Lt Frederick Neilson attached as aide to Mountbatten by the Navy Department, his wife Eulalia who attached herself as aide to Edwina, the Mountbattens, Colonel George Thompson, their host and a great friend of Mountbatten's parents, his niece Mrs Pell, and her husband Steve Pell.

Overleaf
Chaplin took the Mountbattens to see Cecil B. de Mille directing a scene.

Overleaf
The Mountbattens stayed at 'Pickfair' and, in the absence of their friends Mary Pickford and Douglas Fairbanks, Charlie Chaplin was their host.

'Suicide Rock', Grand Canyon: Lt Neilson, his wife and the Mountbattens.

Opposite page
On the plateau 1300 feet from the bottom of the Grand Canyon, the Mountbattens and their guide Jim Stevens.

The Mountbattens had ridden out from the Grand Canyon to an Indian Village.

96

But the highlight of the trip for the couple was Hollywood – the film capital of the world. Films had always fascinated Mountbatten. During his first Tour with the Prince of Wales in 1920 as Flag-Lieutenant in charge of the Signal Department of the *Renown*, he conceived the idea of making use of the ciné-cameraman, embarked for the cruise, to make a film to teach Fleet Manoeuvres. This was the first instructional film ever made in the Services but it was rejected by the Board of Admiralty who said that Their Lordships could see no possible application of film for instructional purposes.

Eighteen years later Mountbatten founded and is still the President of the Royal Naval Film Corporation which arranges to supply films to the sea-going fleet at a price within the reach of all ships' companies. His scheme was copied much later by the Army and Royal Air Force and has proved a great morale factor in Service life.

In 1922 Mountbatten already possessed his own portable 35-mm ciné-camera and now he learnt the art of directing from top directors like Cecil B. de Mille.

Left
Chaplin's present to the young couple was a film 'Nice and Friendly' written and directed by, as well as starring, Charlie Chaplin.
The cast of 'Nice and Friendly'. Steve Pell, Mountbatten, Charlie, Edwina, Freddy Neilson, Eulalia and Colonel Thompson. Absent: Jackie Coogan.

Below: far left
Charlie and Mountbatten remove their make-up.

Shaking hands with the famous baseball player Babe Ruth in New York.

The couple stayed at Pickfair, the home of their friends Mary Pickford and Douglas Fairbanks. They were away, so their partner, Charlie Chaplin, acted as host. He made a film with the young couple as a wedding present which he called 'Nice and Friendly'. He wrote it, directed it and appeared in it in two roles – his normal self and as the little tramp he had made world-famous. Dickie and Edwina were also in the film together with the child actor Jackie Coogan.

As an actor Mountbatten was rather less of a success. In his autobiography Chaplin captioned a still from the film: 'Breaking the news to Lord Mountbatten that he is no actor!'

In December the couple sailed for home after a wonderful adventure. They had dined with Jerome Kern in New York, met Babe Ruth the baseball hero, ridden the Roller Coaster at Coney Island, visited Chicago, Niagara Falls and the Grand Canyon. They left the shores of America having acquired a liking for America and Americans which they never lost.

Mountbatten's sister, Louise, got married the following year. Louise was thirty-four, and had turned down a number of proposals, including a dynastic marriage to King Manoel of Portugal. Now she was courted by the Crown Prince of Sweden, Gustaf Adolf, who had in 1905 married Margaret, Princess of Connaught (Daisy), the elder daughter of Queen Victoria's third son. They had had five children, but Daisy had died in 1920. Louise was dubious, considering herself too old to be a bride; but her mother urged her to accept, and she did. They married on 3 November 1923 in the Chapel Royal at Westminster, with almost as much pomp and as big a crowd of Royalty and ex-Royalty as there had been for Mountbatten's and Edwina's wedding. Their marriage was a very happy one and though Louise's only child was still-born she loved her step-children. She shared her husband's liberal ideas which endeared them to the democratic Swedes. They went skating together, and were to be seen bicycling through the streets.

Mountbatten's own marriage was also to be a very happy one, and on 14 February 1924, exactly two years after they had become engaged in Viceregal Lodge in Delhi, the Mountbattens' daughter Patricia was born at Brook House.

Mountbatten's first child Patricia was christened in the spring of 1924.

Holding her father's right hand
the two-year-old Patricia and
holding the other,
Mountbatten's nephew Prince
Philip. Adsdean 1926.

Patricia at Adsdean aged 2.

Bathing from *Shrimp*.

Noël Coward, a close friend of
the Mountbattens, Gozo 1934.

The Mountbattens on board
their yacht *Shrimp*, Deauville
1926.

Adsdean was a house rented by the Mountbattens from 1924 to 1939. Here with 'Fruity' Metcalfe, the Prince of Wales' Equerry.

The Twenties were getting into full swing; the Mountbattens belonged to the smartest and most glamorous set in Society, and Mountbatten earned an unmerited reputation as a playboy. In fact he was working harder than ever.

This was the period when Britain proudly achieved all speed records on land, on water and in the air. Everybody was rather speed-crazy and Mountbatten was no exception. He possessed a 40-knot motor-boat which got him into bad odour with the Royal Yacht Squadron on several occasions. He was one of the first to take up water-skiing in 1932 and became so proficient he literally used to water-ski to shipboard dinner parties fully clothed but with shoes and socks tied

Douglas Fairbanks and Mary
Pickford were often guests.

Above
Fairbanks and son.

Mountbatten's love of boats extends to motor-boats and *Shadow II* was a favourite in a succession of *Shadows*.

Exchanging caps. The Mountbattens and the Prince of Wales at Cowes.

Watching polo in 1932, the Mountbattens, Yola Letellier and Lt Michael Hodges.

Above: left
Polo learnt in India remained a sport Mountbatten has continued to enjoy throughout his life. Extreme left: Winston Churchill, extreme right: Mountbatten.

The Duke of York presenting the Duke of York Royal Navy/Royal Air Force Cup to the victorious Captain, Ranelagh, July 1933.

round his neck. He was friends with Sir Henry Segrave who held both land and water records. He knew R. J. Mitchell, the aircraft designer, who at that time was building seaplanes to win the Schneider Trophy. On one occasion Mountbatten took him out in his boat, *Shadow II*, to watch his machine at the moment of take-off during trials for the Schneider Cup Race.

As well as fast boats he enjoyed fast cars. In 1924 he drove down in his new Rolls-Royce from Brook House in Park Lane to the gates of Portsmouth Barracks in one hour and thirty-two minutes. That was long before motorways and when four-wheel brakes were scarcely known.

Both he and Edwina had serious sides to their personalities and both were capable of putting in an amazing amount of hard work. And in spite of the parties, this was how Mountbatten spent the next few years of his life – working hard in the service he loved.

A Serving Officer

Mountbatten with two friends
on a stranded water boat at
Anzac Cove, Dardanelles.

In January 1923 Mountbatten
joined the *Revenge*. This group
comprises the Midshipmen,
Petty Officers and Leading
Seamen of Mountbatten's
division.

IN 1923 Mountbatten began to pick up the threads of his naval career. He joined the battleship *Revenge*, then with the International Fleet in the Dardanelles and at Constantinople, and got to know foreign navies and the Allied Army of Occupation.

Mountbatten now had to choose a speciality. He was ambitious and full of good ideas but it was hard to decide what branch of the Navy he was best fitted for. He thought of submarines, of which he had had some experience during the war, but rejected them because they would be less exciting in peace time. Another idea was aviation; in 1918 he had spent his leave learning to fly and enjoyed it. But the Navy no longer had control of the Fleet Air Arm, so he would have had to obtain a commission in the Air Force in order to fly for the Navy, and that did not attract him. In the end he decided on Signals, which turned out to be an excellent choice. He had always had a flair for communications – both in the technical sense and a more general one.

In 1924 Mountbatten went to the Signal School at Portsmouth, and in 1925 he attended the Higher Wireless Course at Greenwich which qualified him to become a member of the Institution of Electrical Engineers. In 1926 he was appointed Reserve Fleet Communications Officer and in 1927 Assistant Fleet Wireless Officer to the Mediterranean Fleet, a most sought-after appointment; but he had earned it by coming out top in the Signal course.

He was based in HMS *Queen Elizabeth*, and so found himself back in Malta. He, Edwina and the new baby took a charming house called Casa Medina, at the top of a very narrow, tortuous road. In 1929 their second daughter Pamela was born in rather extraordinary circumstances. Mountbatten was with the 2nd Destroyer Flotilla visiting Barcelona and Edwina drove herself to meet him. No sooner had she reached Barcelona than the baby began to arrive very suddenly and the only doctor in the hotel where they were staying was a retired throat specialist. Mountbatten put a call through to Madrid to ask his cousin, Queen Ena of Spain, for her advice. She was away and he was put through to King Alfonso who jumped to all the wrong conclusions. 'You're having a baby,' he said. 'How exciting. I'll tell nobody.' Mountbatten pointed out that this was the exact opposite of what they wanted – they needed help. 'Oh very well,' said the King, 'I'll tell the Military Governor.'

Edwina in her two-seater 20 hp Rolls-Royce at Port Lympne when *Revenge* was at Folkestone and Mountbatten was on leave. The Mountbattens were guests of Philip Sassoon.

Right
In 1926 Mountbatten returned to Malta as Assistant Fleet Wireless Officer but there was always time for fancy dress parties. These costumes were provided by their friends Douglas and Mary Fairbanks.

Mountbatten wearing an outfit of his own design. Casa Medina, Malta 1928.

The Military Governor of Barcelona arrived at the hotel in full dress uniform and announced that by the King's orders he was putting sentries round the hotel. All they succeeded in doing was preventing the real doctor from getting in when he did arrive. Despite the confusion, mother and baby were fine but it was certainly a harrowing experience.

Mountbatten found time in Malta to develop his passion for polo. He was, on his own admission, not naturally good at it, but he devoted to it his infinite capacity for taking pains – he had slow-motion films made to analyse the shots, devised a new stick that gave longer and higher shots, and worked out tactics with his team on the billiard table. It seemed a natural sequel to put what he had learned into a book, *Introduction to Polo*, published under the pseudonym 'Marco'. It became a best-seller and continues to sell well and has been translated into several languages.

Between 1929 and 1931 Mountbatten spent some time as Senior Instructor in Wireless Telegraphy at the Signal School in Portsmouth. He threw himself with enjoyment into teaching and lecturing, and also made changes in the tools of instruction: he devised a new way of laying out radio diagrams, so that they were easier to understand, and he wrote the first comprehensive textbook on all the wireless sets used in the Navy.

In 1931 he returned to the Mediterranean as Fleet Wireless Officer, and was responsible for radio communication throughout the seventy ships of the Mediterranean Fleet. One of his special concerns was to improve the image of the wireless telegraphists and show just how important their job was. Yet again, he found himself trying to persuade the senior officers of the Fleet of the importance of modern techniques and ideas. With typical flamboyance, he staged some dramatic demonstrations for the Senior Officer and Signal Officer of the Fleet, showing the necessity of wireless discipline by simulating the situation in battle, with signals coming from aircraft, submarines and the ships themselves.

In November 1932 the BBC announced that King George V would inaugurate the first Empire Broadcasting Service by personally speaking to all his people on Christmas Day. The Commander-in-Chief of the Mediterranean sent for Mountbatten and ordered him to arrange that every man in the Fleet and, if possible, also the Army, RAF and civilians in Malta should hear the King's voice.

Mountbatten explained that there was no service equipment supplied to the Fleet which would make this possible. A new, specially designed H/F Receiver would have to be built on a high point and a cable run to a ship alongside which would transmit the King's words on its M/F transmitter altered to carry voice instead of Morse telegraphy. All other ships would have to use the loud-speaker sets which Mountbatten's technical staff had previously designed when their silent cinema projectors had been converted to sound.

The Commander-in-Chief approved money and manpower. The

An unusual pet was Sabi, the lion cub. Adsdean, 1936.

While commanding HMS *Wishart* Mountbatten invented a new rowing stroke.

Captain of HMS *Wishart*, 1935

equipment was sent by train to Syracuse and fetched, the last vital components arriving on Christmas Eve. On Christmas Day they only picked up the BBC a few minutes before His Majesty spoke but every word was heard by everyone. Five minutes after the King stopped talking the H/F transmission zone beamed on Malta faded right out.

By now Mountbatten was a Commander, due to get what every naval officer wants most – command of a ship. But first he had to do a course at the Naval Tactical School and during it Admiral Jellicoe attended a complete presentation of the Battle of Jutland. Jellicoe made the shocking revelation that at no time had he had a clear idea of what the German High Seas Fleet was doing; no more than four of their twenty-two battleships had been visible at one time, and his own ships had failed to make essential signals or give him useful information about the German Fleet. Mountbatten himself later gave lectures on the Battle of Jutland, and used it to hammer home the vital role of communications in the modern Navy.

In 1934 he was given command of HMS *Daring*, one of the most modern destroyers in the Mediterranean Fleet. The whole crew was extremely proud of the ship, and Mountbatten did everything he could to enhance their identification with her: he put up a motto, 'We have made every sea the highway of our daring', and told them '*Daring* by name and daring by nature – that's us.' As his first command the ship meant a great deal to him too: 'The captain's feelings, of course, are absolutely special. You have forty thousand horse-power under your hand. You can move her wherever you want. You must navigate her

through all dangers. Your power is absolute . . . so you are father and mother and God Almighty to every man in the ship. And you get paid – for doing the most wonderful job in the world!'

After a few months, however, they received orders to exchange ships with the China Destroyer Flotilla, and Mountbatten found himself with an old ship, the *Wishart*, not nearly such a glorious name. But Mountbatten had to rekindle the ship's company's enthusiasm so he made just the right kind of speech to achieve this: 'We have just left behind a ship with a great name – the *Daring*: a wonderful name. We have come to the only ship in the Navy with a greater name. For our ship is called after the Almighty Himself, to whom we pray every day: "Our Father Wishart in Heaven . . ."'

The only real outlet for his energy at this time was to make the *Wishart* the best of the thirty-six destroyers in the Mediterranean Fleet. The *Wishart* went on to win practically every trophy in the Command, including those for gunnery, cricket, football, water polo and communications exercises. Mountbatten invented a new stroke for rowing, cutting the beginning and end of the stroke and speeding up the effective middle part from 32 to 40 strokes a minute and was himself stroke of the Officers' Whaler. He came in for some criticism for being unsportsmanlike – he was accused of ruining the 'style' of rowing and, in gunnery practice, of firing at too slow a rate: fast shooting was a fetish in destroyers at that time. But the scoring was on hits per minute, not speed of firing, and it seemed obvious to him that 'the best thing for guns to do is to hit their targets'.

Pamela and Patricia in 1936.

Patricia at Adsdean, 1936.

Patricia, Mountbatten holding the pet bush baby 'Bozo', Pamela and Edwina.

Pamela with her mother in Malta, 1935.

All this was enjoyable, but many in the peace-time Navy soon began to realize that another war was a distinct possibility. On 2 October 1935 Italy invaded Abyssinia, the first of the aggressive moves by dictators that led up to the Second World War. The Mediterranean Fleet was strongly reinforced to meet a possible challenge from the Italian Navy. Its base was transferred from Malta to Alexandria, though the 1st Destroyer Flotilla, to which the *Wishart* belonged, was left behind in Malta. They called themselves 'the death or glory boys'.

Edwina stayed in Malta as the other naval wives left. Neither she nor Mountbatten doubted that another war was approaching. Mountbatten was recalled to England to an appointment in the Naval Air Division for, although he never qualified as a Service pilot, he had a long history of flying experience. Not only had he been up in an airship when he was six and flown as a passenger in the first Naval Short biplane when he was eleven, but in 1918 he had spent his leave learning to fly with the newly formed Royal Air Force. He had proved an apt pupil but could not be granted 'Wings' as his course was unofficial.

The Road to War

THE Silver Jubilee in May 1935 had been the occasion for a spontaneous outburst of affection by the people of Great Britain for their King, George V. The King was amazed to find that he was so well loved and remarked, 'I'd no idea they felt like that about me, I'm beginning to think they must really like me for myself!'

Sadly, the King's health deteriorated rapidly, and on 20 January 1936 he died and many feared that stability and democracy would die with him. Mountbatten respected and admired the King but was never close to him. George V was a distinctly awe-inspiring figure to the younger members of his family, and more of a 'Victorian' than his own father, Edward VII.

The Prince of Wales, on the other hand, who now became King Edward VIII, was Mountbatten's best friend as well as being a cousin. The two young men shared a joy of life and dislike of pompous protocol which made them suspect to the older generation but much loved by the ordinary people. The new King's sympathy with the unemployed, war-wounded and the victims of social oppression was demonstrably genuine. The new reign began with the brightest hopes.

In November 1936, however, Prime Minister Baldwin was faced with the King's openly expressed desire to marry Mrs Wallis Simpson, an American lady previously married to Lt Winfield Spencer of the United States Navy. Her divorce from her second husband had come through in October, and as a divorced woman she could not be crowned Queen or even married in the Church of England. But the King was determined, and said he would prefer to abdicate if the constitutional objections to his marriage proved insuperable.

Wallis Simpson and the King often met the Mountbattens, and the King's decision was no surprise to them. While recognizing what it meant to the King to love Wallis Simpson, Mountbatten was opposed to his abdication, convinced that his duty to his country came first.

The burden on Prince Albert, the Duke of York, who felt himself unprepared to become King in place of his brother, was considerable, and Mountbatten could only encourage him by telling him what his father, Prince Louis, had said to the Duke's father on the death of his older brother: that a naval training was the best possible preparation for being a King. King Edward VIII summoned his three brothers and Mountbatten to spend his last afternoon at Fort Belvedere with him. He abdicated on 10 December 1936, and the Duke of York mounted

The Mountbattens got to know Mrs Simpson well. Monte Carlo 1935.

The Duke and Duchess of York at about this time.

Mountbatten, the King in 'rural dress' and, second from the end, Wallis Simpson arm in arm with Edwina. Balmoral, August 1936.

Right
Wallis Simpson, Mountbatten and the King, August 1936.

Below: left
Playing 'Arrow Golf'.

The King, Mountbatten, Esmond Harmsworth, Wallis Simpson (third from right) and Edwina (far right).

Mountbatten and Princess
Elizabeth on board the Royal
yacht *Victoria and Albert* at the
Coronation Naval Review, May 1937.

Mountbatten, King George VI,
Princess Elizabeth and the Duke
of Kent.

Left to right: Princess Elizabeth,
Mountbatten, the Duke of Kent
and Queen Elizabeth.

Princess Elizabeth and
Mountbatten.

the throne as King George VI. He was crowned at Westminster Abbey on 12 May 1937.

The years leading up to the Second World War held a series of personal losses for the family; 1937 was a particularly black year. Mountbatten's much loved Uncle Ernie's younger son, Prince Louis of Hesse (Lu) had become engaged to an English girl, the Hon. Margaret Geddes. They planned to marry on 23 October 1937 but the Grand Duke's health was failing, and he died on 9 October. The wedding was postponed for a month.

Grand Duke Ernest-Louis' older son, Prince George Donatus (Don), the hereditary Grand Duke of Hesse, was due to fly to England with his family four days before the wedding. Prince George had married a cousin: his wife was Victoria's granddaughter, Princess Cecile of Greece, one of the four daughters of Mountbatten's sister Alice. Don and Cecile had three children, two of whom accompanied them on the

In the spring of 1938 'Georgie', Mountbatten's brother died. King George VI and the Duke of Kent walk behind Midshipman David now third Marquess of Milford Haven. Alongside David is Mountbatten and in front of them are being carried the late Marquess's decorations.

trip, and Cecile was expecting another. Also with them was Ernie's widow, the Grand Duchess Eleanor. The aeroplane crashed while trying to land in fog at Ostend, and everyone on board was killed. The only survivor of the family, the youngest, Princess Johanna, died eighteen months later.

In 1938 the Mountbatten family suffered an even greater loss. Georgie, the second Marquess of Milford Haven, died of cancer at the early age of forty-six. Mountbatten had worshipped his older brother and greatly respected his brilliant mind. 'He was the sort of person who, instead of reading detective stories, would sit down and read problems of higher calculus, and solve them in his head', he remembers. Georgie used to work out complicated gunnery problems in his head, astonishing his brother officers. As well as being clever, he was an extremely kind man. The Queen remembers finding herself next to him at the wedding breakfast of the Duke of Kent and Princess Marina, when she was only eight; he talked to her charmingly and seriously as though she were grown up. Georgie was buried with full Naval Honours and King George VI and the Duke of Kent both walked in the funeral procession.

In his new job at the Naval Air Division, Mountbatten found himself at the centre of the political arguments that were raging as Hitler and Mussolini perpetrated more and more aggressive acts – especially the split between those who favoured appeasement, and those who knew war was inevitable and urged rearmament before it was too late. He himself, though recoiling like everyone else from the horrors of another war, was firmly of the latter opinion. His job was to help try to persuade the Government to bring control of the Fleet Air Arm back to the Navy; at present its control was divided between the Admiralty and the Air Ministry.

At the same time he tried as hard as he could to convince the Government that the Navy's air services were frighteningly out of date and that rearmament in all the Services was essential. But there was a curious blindness among politicians to the implications of Hitler's manoeuvres. In 1936 he pointed out to Mr Baldwin at a dinner party given by King Edward VIII that the Germans were building numerous airfields in north-west Germany, and that this implied plans to attack England but Baldwin was uninterested.

In 1937 Stanley Baldwin retired and Neville Chamberlain became Prime Minister. Appeasement was now an active policy and few people opposed it. Churchill, the leader of the anti-appeasement group, was out of office. In 1938, Hitler demanded the annexation of Sudetenland, and on 27 September the Royal Navy was mobilized in preparation for war. But at Munich Neville Chamberlain obtained his worthless piece of paper and war was postponed, while Czechoslovakia was left in Hitler's hands. Duff Cooper, First Lord of the Admiralty, who was strongly anti-appeasement and had been largely responsible for the mobilization of the Navy, resigned in protest and Mountbatten could not refrain from writing to congratulate him on his courage.

With war looming the whole family gets into uniform.

After Munich rearmament did begin, though slowly. The Navy succeeded in winning back control of the Fleet Air Arm, helped by Mountbatten's strenuous efforts. Mountbatten was concerned at the Navy's lack of protection against low-flying aircraft attacks, and did his best to persuade the Gunnery Division that new anti-aircraft guns were needed, although it was not really his business. He pointed out that machine guns firing solid bullets were largely ineffective and pom-poms too slow and cumbersome. He advised a 20-millimetre cannon firing explosive shells very rapidly. He found the right gun for the job – the Swiss Oerlikon – and even had one fitted on a new motor torpedo boat that was being built as a private venture; but when the Admiralty bought the boat, they did so on condition that the new gun was removed. They did not even want to try it. Eventually, in despair, he went directly to the First Sea Lord, Admiral Backhouse, under whom he had served during the war, and convinced him. The Oerlikon gun was immediately adopted and eventually became standard equipment in the Fleets.

As so often in his life, Mountbatten was faced with the innate conservatism of men in administration. In 1936 he had made friends with a French scientist, Robert Esnault Pelterie, who foretold the coming of rocket missiles within ten years – and also rockets to the moon within thirty years. Mountbatten handed this man's work on rocket missiles to the Admiralty, but thinks that no use whatever was made of it, as those concerned could not understand French. Another, more urgent technical advance was in the encoding of messages. For some time after the outbreak of war, the Navy's old-fashioned cypher system enabled the Germans to read all their messages. Mountbatten pressed in 1936 for a changeover to mechanical encypherment and even got the controller of the Navy to buy four Typex Cypher machines, developed by the RAF but the Fleet rejected cypher machines until after the outbreak of war. As a result many lives were lost.

In 1938 Mountbatten had been selected for the Higher Commanders' Course at Aldershot and he got to know many of the generals he was to have dealings with in the coming war, in particular General Sir Claude Auchinleck, who was leader of Mountbatten's Syndicate.

In 1939 Mountbatten was appointed Captain (D) commanding the 5th Destroyer Flotilla. These were all brand-new ships of the 'J' and 'K' Class and Mountbatten's own ship, the flotilla leader, HMS *Kelly*, was handed over to him by the builders, Hawthorne Leslie, on 23 August 1939, ten days before war broke out.

The *Kelly* was named after Admiral Sir John Kelly and was launched by his daughter. The *Kelly* quickly became a happy and efficient ship. Teamwork enabled commissioning time to be cut from three weeks to three days. 'No one was to take their clothes off or turn in until the job was done. Nobody did, and we finished in three days flat,' recalls Mountbatten.

One of the *Kelly*'s first missions was to go to Cherbourg to bring

On the bridge of HMS *Kelly*.

back the Duke and Duchess of Windsor to Portsmouth. In December 1939 Mountbatten was ordered to collect every available destroyer in the Tyne to search for a submarine which was believed to have torpedoed four ships at the mouth of the river. Mountbatten got in touch with the local Admiral to protest. He pointed out that the scent would be stale and the U-boat miles away in any case. If she had laid mines the leading destroyer was bound to hit one and go up. He was told not to argue but carry out orders so he went well ahead of the rest into the suspected minefields as ordered. *Kelly* hit a mine which fortunately did not explode until hit by the propellers but she had to be towed back to be repaired.

Page 2.

Surname *Mountbatten*

Other Names *The Lord Louis GCVO, ADC.*

Rank (at time of issue) *Captain RN.*

Ship (at time of issue) *Iris, Kelly*

Place of Birth *Windsor*

Year of Birth *1900*

Issued by *The Captain (D)*

At *IMMINGHAM*

Date *15th June 1940*

Page 3.
Navy Form S.1511

NAVAL
IDENTITY CARD No. 14061

THE CAPTAIN
15 JUN
FIFTH DESTROYER

Signature of Bearer

Louis Mountbatten

Visible distinguishing marks

Cross on forehead

The Naval Identity Card which Mountbatten had in his wallet when *Kelly* went down.

Torpedoed in the night of 10 May 1940, Mountbatten after ninety hours on the bridge brings *Kelly* home.

Only one man panicked and left his post, the penalty for which was death. Mountbatten chose to caution the man instead of punishing him. As he told the ship's company, 'I propose letting him off with a caution – or rather two cautions: one to him, and one to me, for having failed to impress myself sufficiently in three months on all of you, for you to know that I would never tolerate such behaviour. Nobody will ever again leave their post. I will never give the order, "Abandon Ship". The only way in which we will ever leave the ship will be if she sinks under our feet.'

The next time the *Kelly* was in trouble, she seemed likely to do just that. During the Norwegian Campaign she was ordered to intercept and destroy some German minelayers, and while speeding to her destination was hit by a torpedo. Mountbatten's nephew, Lord Milford Haven, was in the *Kandahar* next astern, and asked his Captain if they could stop and pick up survivors from the *Kelly*. He was assured that there could be no survivors from such an explosion. Luckily the *Bulldog*, a destroyer from another flotilla, arrived and took the *Kelly* in tow.

The torpedoed HMS *Kelly*.

Mountbatten takes up the story:

'It was the beginning of a very long haul. First we jettisoned every bit of topweight that we could move. We shot off ten torpedoes and all our depth-charges; we cut our boats adrift; we threw ammunition overboard; we unbolted the lockers, and threw them out too. And so we were able to remain afloat with a heavy list to starboard – rather unsteady, difficult to manage, but the *Kelly* was afloat, and that was all that mattered to me.

'I remained on the bridge for the whole of our return trip. Late the first night, we suddenly heard the sound of an E-boat engine, and then she arrived at full speed. She hit the *Bulldog* a glancing blow, bounced off her and came right inboard onto the *Kelly*. Our starboard gunwale was awash, and so she was able to come right on board us with a rush, firing her 20 mm gun. I remember ducking down behind the bridge screen and thinking to myself: "What a damn silly thing to do!" So I straightened up and watched the rest of the action. The E-boat (*MTB40*, we now know it was) shored off davits and guard rails as she passed down *Kelly*'s side, and then vanished into the night.

'And then came the Luftwaffe. We were transferring our wounded to the *Kandahar* when they first appeared. The first attack was driven off, but we knew they would be back – and they were. We buried our dead at sea – as many of them as we could extract from the wreckage – and that was an eerie and harrowing experience; I had to read the Burial Service while helm orders were passed down the ship: "Ashes to ashes . . . starboard ten . . . dust to dust . . . midships . . ."

'By now there were quite a few ships clustered round us, and the Admiral signalled me saying that with Hitler invading the Low Countries this was a waste of force; he suggested that we should open the seacocks and scuttle the *Kelly*. To this I replied that I did not wish to scuttle my ship; we could dispense with further help and defend ourselves if tugs could be sent to tow us.

'So in due course a tug arrived to bring us home. But the night before she appeared, we were nearly done for after all; the sea got up, and the ship started to develop a very unpleasant slow roll. I could feel that we were very near complete loss of stability. I racked my brains to think of more topweight that I could get rid of. And then I had a brainwave:

'"The ship's company. They weigh a hell of a lot. Let's get rid of the ship's company!"

'So the whole ship's company was transferred to the escorting destroyers, with the Luftwaffe bombing the open boats as they went across. The next morning the tug appeared, and we were on the last lap. Six officers and twelve men came back aboard – just enough to handle the ship and man the close-range weapons. I worked a 5-inch multiple machine-gun, and I must say that it's much more satisfactory actually firing a gun than just sitting there when you are being attacked!

'And so we came home, after ninety-two hours in tow: home to Hawthorne Leslie's yard at Hebburn, and I'll never forget the heart-warming cheer from all the shipyard workers as we came into the Tyne.'

It was soon after this that one Admiral at a press conference in answer to a question remarked of Mountbatten: 'I know of nobody I'd sooner be with in a tight corner than Dickie Mountbatten, and I know of nobody who could get me into one quicker.'

While the *Kelly* was being repaired, Mountbatten continued to command the flotilla from other destroyers, which went on to carry out bombardments at Cherbourg and later Benghazi, and fought in day and night actions against enemy destroyers. In a night action of November 1940 the ship he was in, the *Javelin*, had her bow and stern blown off by a salvo of torpedoes but again he got her under tow, this time to Devonport.

In November 1940 the *Kelly* was recommissioned and as many of her old company as were available rejoined her. Mountbatten made his usual speech: '*Kelly* will always steam at full speed to the sound of the guns.' Then she sailed to do her 'working-up' at Scapa Flow. The coastal route to Scapa was reported clear. Suddenly gun flashes and the sound of gunfire disturbed the night. Mountbatten had just been in a battle with German destroyers raiding Channel shipping at night. As the coast had been reported clear it could only be the enemy.

He called his officers together. 'I must carry out my boast and go full speed to the gunfire but as the crew know nothing you must go round and show them how to load and fire the guns and torpedoes; and the Engine Room must increase speed slowly and carefully.' He then sounded the alarm rattlers and said to the Quarter Master, 'Steer to the gun flashes, put the telegraph to "Full Speed".'

Luckily it turned out that a British destroyer leaving a convoy escort early was practising star shell fire without permission so that *Kelly* survived to fight another day.

In 1941 *Kelly* was sent to the Mediterranean, where things were hotting-up and in May, after having sunk the last of the 'caique' invasion fleet and successfully bombarded Maleme airfield in Crete, the *Kelly* was herself attacked by twenty-four Junkers 87 dive-bombers (Stukas) during the Battle of Crete, and turned over at 34 knots. When she was right over Mountbatten climbed on to the distance-correction indicator of the station-keeping device which he had invented and which was fitted throughout his flotilla. With the sea swirling over the bridge and unable to hold on any longer, he took a deep breath. The sea closed over him. As he broke the surface, the stern of the *Kelly* passed him, propellers still revolving, only a few yards away. More than half the *Kelly*'s officers and men were lost. The oil-smeared and burnt survivors, with only one raft to cling to, were machine-gunned in the water, though they found voice to cheer the *Kelly* as she finally went down. The *Kashmir*, her sister ship, was sunk in the same attack, but she went down more slowly than the *Kelly* and in an upright position, so there were five rafts of survivors.

The third ship of the party, the *Kipling*, had had to drop out of the expedition with a steering failure but her Captain saw the dive-bombing and courageously came to pick up as many survivors as he could. Mountbatten recalls:

> '*Kipling* actually nudged the *Kelly* in the water as she went down, and sustained some damage, but it was not important. Then she lowered scrambling nets and we all swam to her. I towed a badly wounded man, but by the time I got to the *Kipling* he was dead and I let go of him. When I got aboard I went up on the bridge, but beyond asking him to go over and collect the survivors of the *Kashmir*, I naturally did not interfere with commander St Clair Ford in the handling of his ship.'

Picking up the *Kashmir*'s survivors was not easy; it took more than three hours, and the *Kipling* and the men in the water were bombarded and machine-gunned by Ju-88s throughout. The *Kipling* had to manoeuvre ceaselessly to avoid being hit. Twice members of Mountbatten's staff suggested that the safety of the ship and the men on board was more important than that of the dwindling number of survivors, and they ought to turn for Alexandria as soon as possible. Both times he refused. Eventually they did head home, though the damaged *Kipling* could only do 17 knots. The ship was attacked again and again, and Mountbatten counted more than eighty near-misses.

When the bombers left off, the ship ran out of fuel. But the *Protector* came out to meet her and she refuelled, and at last arrived in Alexandria. A number of the rescued had died, and only forty to fifty from the *Kelly* were unwounded. As the *Kipling* came into Alexandria, the companies of the Mediterranean Fleet cheered her in. Mountbatten was greeted at the landing stage by his nephew, Prince Philip, a midshipman aboard the *Valiant*, who teased him about his grimy appearance, accusing him of looking like a black and white minstrel.

The story of the *Kelly* during the first twenty-one months of the war was told by Mountbatten's great friend Noël Coward in his film *In Which We Serve*. 'The Master' played the Captain – under a different name – and he also changed the name of the ship at Mountbatten's request. He placed the ship in situations, like Dunkirk, where the *Kelly* had not been present, but it was Mountbatten's cap that Coward wore and Mountbatten's words he used in the dramatic moments of the story.

Against the background of other heroic events in the war, the story of the *Kelly* is not particularly remarkable, but what singled her out was the high morale of the ship's company. So great was it that surviving members formed a Reunion Association which now meets regularly at a dinner, which is organized completely by the men, officers being invited as their guests. Such an Association run by survivors of a destroyed ship's company is without precedent and is a great tribute to Mountbatten's powers of leadership in war.

The Mediterranean Fleet cheers HMS *Kipling* bringing back survivors from the *Kelly* and *Kashmir*.

Survivors from the *Kelly* and *Kashmir*.

Combined Operations

AFTER the *Kelly* had been sunk, and much of the rest of the flotilla, Mountbatten was appointed to command the aircraft-carrier *Illustrious*, then being repaired in the USA following damage in action off Malta. While the ship was refitting, he was invited by the Chief of United States Naval Operations to visit the US Pacific Fleet in Pearl Harbor and give lectures on war at sea to their officers. He also went to sea in an American aircraft-carrier and destroyer leader, and made many valuable contacts in the US Navy. The Americans were not yet at war, though Churchill and Roosevelt had signed the Atlantic Charter in August, bringing American and British policy closer together. Mountbatten was appalled at the vulnerability of Pearl Harbor to a surprise attack, and said so. His fears were pooh-poohed by some senior officers, though the Commander-in-Chief, Admiral Kimmel, agreed with him and forwarded his recommendations.

It was during this visit to the United States in October 1941 that he was recalled by Winston Churchill to succeed Admiral of the Fleet Lord Keyes (on whose staff he had served as a young Lieutenant in 1927) as Adviser on Combined Operations. After informing him of his new appointment, Winston Churchill said he hoped he appreciated its importance. Mountbatten replied, 'Sir, I would sooner be back at sea with my friends.' Winston turned on him and said, 'Have you no sense of glory? I offer you a chance to take part in the highest direction of the war and all you want is to go back to sea. What could you hope to achieve except to be sunk in a bigger and more expensive ship?'

The Prime Minister then went on to explain that Mountbatten's task was twofold; to continue the Commando raids, in order to keep up the offensive spirit, to gain essential experience, and to harass the enemy, but above all he was to prepare in every possible way for the great counter-invasion of Europe. He told Mountbatten he must prepare the plans, order the necessary landing ships and landing-craft, and devise and design all the appurtenances and appliances needed for a successful landing against enemy opposition, and ended by saying, 'I want you to turn the south coast of England from a bastion of defence into a springboard for attack.'

A month later, in November 1941, Mountbatten was ordered, together with the Commander-in-Chief Home Forces, to prepare for a large-scale raid, and then in January 1942 they were told to plan for Allied permanent re-entry into the Continent, in conjunction with other senior British, American and Canadian Generals and Air Marshals who became known as 'the Combined Commanders'. The destruction by the Japanese of so much of the American Fleet in its base at Pearl Harbor on 7 December 1941 had brought America into the war, and though some people saw Pearl Harbor as a crippling blow, Churchill and Mountbatten thought differently: the full backing of American manpower and production could now be called upon.

In December 1941, Combined Operations carried out its first raid under Mountbatten's direction. On Boxing Day a combined force of a cruiser and four destroyers, some 600 Commandos and a few RAF squadrons set out to attack the islands of Vagsoy and Maloy in South Norway, and another force the Lofoten Islands in the north. The raids were successful. Fish-oil factories, a power station, wireless stations and coastal defences were demolished. A number of Germans were killed and captured and some 15,000 tons of shipping were destroyed, with only light British casualties. They were only small raids but their significance was considerable, for this was the first time that all three Services had co-operated in this way and it showed what could be done.

Then in February 1942 Combined Operations pulled off another small but completely successful raid under the noses of the Germans. It was the first successful raid using parachute troops, who were dropped by the RAF on the cliff-top at Bruneval, to the north-east of Le Havre. The paratroops demolished the German radar station, captured vital elements of equipment and brought them safely back across a beach held by commando-trained soldiers to the awaiting naval assault landing-craft. Not only did the success of this raid enable British scientists to evaluate the new Würzburg German radar, but its effect on morale was out of all proportion to the size of the raid and we now know that it infuriated Hitler.

In March 1942 Mountbatten was given the acting rank of Vice-Admiral at the age of forty-one (two years younger than Nelson) and the honorary ranks of Lieutenant-General and Air Marshal, the first time that an actual serving officer had held ranks in all three services. He was made Chief of Combined Operations and became the fourth member of the British Chiefs of Staff Committee, who were responsible for the military conduct of the war.

He was a generation younger than his colleagues on the COS Committee; indeed the First Sea Lord, Sir Dudley Pound, had been his Captain in the battle-cruiser *Repulse* in 1921 when he was a very young Lieutenant. Nevertheless, in spite of the difference in age and substantive rank, they treated him as an equal. A naval historian, Commander Kenneth Edwards, remarked in 1943 that all this was not necessarily to his advantage: 'He has in effect been lifted out of his generation, and unless he can revert to the rank of Captain and be given a command at sea his subsequent naval career may be cut unduly short.'

On 28 March 1942, ten days after his 'promotion', Combined Operations carried out their biggest and most dramatic raid so far on St

Nazaire. The object of the raid was to put out of action the great dry dock in St Nazaire harbour which was the only one on the Atlantic coast big enough to take the giant German battleship *Tirpitz*. The plan was to ram the gate of the dock with an old destroyer, *Campbeltown*, crammed with high explosive and a delayed action fuse. It was a most hazardous voyage, entailing a long run-in under heavy fire, but the destroyer made it. Torpedoes were fired into the harbour installations and Commandos landed and carried out more demolitions. The next day, after the raid was over, and the *Campbeltown* was crowded with German officers inspecting her, the ship exploded. This daring and courageous operation, in which no less than five VCs were won, ensured that the *Tirpitz* never attempted to come into the Atlantic.

In April 1942 Harry Hopkins, personal adviser to President Roosevelt, and General George Marshall, Chief of Staff of the US Army, arrived in London to discuss American plans with the British Government and Chiefs of Staff. During this visit General Marshall asked to come and visit the Combined Operations Headquarters and, as a result, the US Chiefs of Staff sent officers of their three services to join the staff of Mountbatten. The Combined Operations Headquarters thus became the first integrated inter-allied, inter-service Headquarters in history and the forerunner of all that followed later in the war. Marshall and Mountbatten agreed that US Rangers should be raised based on the British Commandos and trained at the Commando School at Achnacarry in Scotland. The strength of the Command rose to 50,000 officers and other ranks of the three services, including the largest number of Wrens in a single Command.

On 19 August 1942 a one-day raid (*Jubilee*) was carried out against the enemy in Dieppe. This raid was sponsored by the Chief of Combined Operations because he had at last got enough landing-craft to lift one division and needed to gain experience of an assault on a port before the detailed planning for the Invasion (*Overlord*) was started. The plan included the capture of the port and the sending in of a 'cutting-out' party on board coastal craft and tank landing-craft three hours after the assault. They were to 'cut out' barges suitable for use by the Allied Invasion forces and tow them back to England.

This raid has been described by people who do not understand what it achieved as a catastrophe. The losses were disturbing, but Dieppe taught the planners lessons which had to be learnt. At a briefing meeting prior to the raid, Winston Churchill turned to Mountbatten's chief Naval planner, Captain Jock Hughes-Hallett, and asked whether he could guarantee success. The Chief of the Imperial General Staff, Field Marshal Alan Brooke, told Hughes-Hallett not to reply and said: 'If he, or anyone else, could guarantee success there would indeed be no object in doing the operation. It is just because no one has the slightest idea what the outcome will be that the operation is necessary.' Winston Churchill replied that this was not a moment at which he wanted to be taught by adversity. 'In that case,' said Alan Brooke, 'you must abandon the idea of invading France because no responsible General will be associated with any planning for invasion until we have an operation at least the size of the Dieppe raid behind us to study and base our plans upon.' This dramatic confrontation made it quite clear that the invasion hung on the raid.

The COHQ staff put up a pincer movement plan, designed on Mountbatten's instructions to avoid a frontal assault. The CIGS insisted that as a Canadian Division was involved (which was a political decision) the Land Forces planning should be done under the direction of Home Forces, who objected to the COHQ plan and said it must be a frontal assault. In June 1942 Mountbatten was sent by the Prime Minister to Washington to discuss future high level strategy with the President and US Joint Chiefs of Staff. During his absence it was decided at a meeting of the Force Commanders under General Montgomery to forego the maximum intensity bombing attack, mainly because the Army feared the bombing would clutter the streets with debris and impede the movement of British tanks, and to enable the 'cutting-out' parties to perform their task it was necessary to avoid damage to the harbour installation and the power house. On his return from America Mountbatten protested to the CIGS who insisted that the Force Commanders must be allowed to have their way.

One of the lessons learnt at Dieppe was the need for overwhelming fire support. It was the inadequacy of the bombardment support which prevented the capture of the port, yet full and overwhelming bombardment would have destroyed the port facilities. This experience reinforced the conclusion which Mountbatten had already come to: that the only way to have a port intact in an invasion was to bring over a prefabricated mobile port. From this idea were born the famous 'Mulberry' artificial harbours, which ultimately played such a vital part in the D-Day operations.

Roosevelt and Churchill met at Casablanca in January 1943. Mountbatten with the three other members of the Chiefs of Staff Committee.

On Mountbatten's right:
General Ismay.

In preparation for the invasion, Mountbatten asked one of his scientists, Solly Zuckerman (now Lord Zuckerman), to produce what was called the 'Interdiction plan'. This was intended to prevent the enemy moving reinforcements against the landing during the dangerous period of the build-up. Solly Zuckerman suggested that the Air Force should bomb all the rolling stock, bridges and tunnels along the German lines of communication, thus keeping their reinforcements out of the invasion area. The 'bomber barons', who had their own strategy of air power, were very opposed to this but General Eisenhower saw the point and forced it through.

During the following months, as the date of the invasion drew nearer, Combined Operations Headquarters was a hive of activity.

Into it flowed a seemingly endless stream of ideas, some of which – like *Pluto*, the 'Pipe-Line Under The Ocean' which carried petrol to the Normandy beach-head – were brilliant.

In November 1942 came the largest Combined Operations yet seen – Operation *Torch*, the allied landing in North Africa – for which Mountbatten's COHQ staff prepared the assault plans. This was carried out successfully and by May 1943 the Axis Powers were beaten in Africa. More Combined Operations followed and two months later, in July 1943, the Allies invaded Sicily, again using assault plans prepared by COHQ, causing the downfall of Mussolini.

By this time a new organization had been set up under Lieutenant-General Frederick Morgan who had been appointed Chief of Staff to the future Supreme Allied Commander (COSSAC), and the detailed preparation for D-Day became his responsibility. General Morgan found his position as the Chief of Staff to an unnamed Supreme Allied Commander did not give him the necessary authority to make decisions. He and his staff had not yet accepted that *Overlord* could be carried out successfully at all and, even if it could, they were undecided whether to land in the Pas de Calais area, which was favoured by the majority of the Combined Commanders' Committee, or to back Mountbatten's obstinately held view that the landing must be in the Normandy area.

This had been a bone of contention for some time. From the start, all the Allied Generals and Air Marshals had been in favour of the invasion taking place in the Pas de Calais area. Mountbatten alone had resolutely and ceaselessly opposed them, pressing for the Normandy area. He pointed out the formidable coast defences developed by the Germans in the Pas de Calais area, which could dominate the Straits of Dover. At the Combined Commanders' meetings Mountbatten repeatedly argued his case, and was at pains to show that the continental Channel ports from Le Havre to the eastward were all shallow ports with narrow entrances, capable of complete obstruction by minefields. On the other hand, the ports to the westward, notably Cherbourg, were deep-water ports with wide entrances which could not be so easily mined, and were not so well defended. This, coupled with our local command of the sea in the Western area, demanded an attack in the Baie de la Seine.

Mountbatten came to the rescue of General Morgan by holding a conference (*Rattle*) at one of his establishments in Scotland, Largs. As a result of this conference, General Morgan put up plans for the landing to take place in the Baie de la Seine which were fully accepted by General Eisenhower on his appointment as Supreme Allied Commander in December 1943. Hitler's Generals shared the same view as the Allied Generals and moved twenty-five divisions to the Pas de Calais area. The Allies were able to put up a credible deception that they meant to land in the Calais area, which kept the enemy forces and strong defences concentrated in the wrong place.

Having completed his part in the plans and preparations for the

In the *Queen Mary* on the way
to the Quebec Conference of
August 1943. Left to right:
Mountbatten, Portal, Churchill,
Brooke, Pound.

With Winston Churchill after
the announcement that
Mountbatten was now Supreme
Allied Commander South East
Asia. August 1943.

invasion of Europe, Mountbatten had high hopes of returning to sea in command of a ship. But Churchill thwarted his desires yet again. In August 1943 Mountbatten accompanied the Prime Minister and the other three Chiefs of Staff to the Allied Conference in Quebec. It was here, walking up and down the battlements overlooking the Heights of Abraham, that Winston Churchill offered Mountbatten the job of Supreme Allied Commander South East Asia. When the Prime Minister asked him what he thought of the idea, Mountbatten replied: 'May I have twenty-four hours to think it over?' 'Why?' Churchill asked. 'Are you afraid you can't do the job?' 'Not at all,' Mountbatten replied, 'I have a congenital weakness for feeling certain I can do anything, but I do want to ask the British and US Chiefs of Staff to satisfy myself that they agree with your choice wholeheartedly and will back me to the full.' When Mountbatten found that he had their full backing, and above all President Roosevelt's, he accepted at once.

It was thus, after two years of long hard preparations for the invasion of Europe, sometimes working up to sixteen hours a day, that Mountbatten was to find himself on the other side of the world when D-Day finally came in June 1944. But all that he had accomplished so successfully in his two years as Chief of Combined Operations was vindicated on 12 June 1944 when Churchill, Field Marshal Smuts (Prime Minister of South Africa), Field Marshal Sir Alan Brooke (Chairman of the British Chiefs of Staff's Committee) and the three US Chiefs of Staff, General Marshall (Army), General Arnold (Air Force) and Admiral King (Navy), visited the landing beaches and on return sent the following signal to him in his South East Asia HQ:

'Today we visited the British and American Armies on the soil of France. We sailed through vast fleets of ships with landing-craft of many types pouring more men, vehicles and stores ashore. We saw clearly the manoeuvre in process of rapid development. We have shared our secrets in common and helped each other all we could. We wish to tell you at this moment in your arduous campaign that we realize that much of this remarkable technique, and therefore the success of the venture, has its origin in developments effected by you and your Staff of Combined Operations. Signed: Arnold, Marshall, King, Brooke, Smuts, Churchill.'

There is little doubt that Mountbatten's outstanding powers of initiative and leadership, his ability to work on terms of close friendship with other nationalities, and above all his resoluteness in insisting that the landings must take place on the Normandy beaches, made possible, thirty years later, the celebrations in Arromanches commemorating the successful invasion of Europe. It is little wonder that this small town has an 'Avenue Amiral Mountbatten'.

Supreme Commander

IN August 1943, Mountbatten took up his new appointment. The job to be done in South East Asia was a difficult one.

There had been good news for the Allies on many fronts; the Axis was beaten in Africa and in July 1943 the Allies had invaded Sicily; Mussolini fell a fortnight later. On the Eastern Front there had been a series of successful Russian offensives but in the Far East the Imperial Japanese armies seemed unstoppable. After Pearl Harbor in 1941 they captured Hong Kong and attacked Malaya. On 15 February 1942 Britain's great Far Eastern base at Singapore had capitulated to the Japanese, who took 85,000 prisoners. During 1942 they had captured Rangoon and advanced northwards through Burma to the very frontier of India.

The morale of the Allied troops in the Far East was low. The myth of the 'invincible Jap' terrorized them; he had seemingly miraculous powers of endurance and a ferocious determination to kill or be killed. Japanese soldiers hardly ever surrendered. Their Emperor was a god to them and death in his service was the noblest end they could desire – as was demonstrated dramatically by the Kamikaze pilots, who flew suicide missions against the American and British fleets, dropping their planes, themselves and a full load of bombs where they would do most damage.

In October 1943 Mountbatten arrived in Delhi. The troops under his command were mainly Indian – British and Gurkhas – but they included Chinese, Americans, Africans, Australians, Burmese, French and Dutch. To weld these, the Navies and the Air Forces of the Allies, over a million strong, into a co-ordinated entity with the morale to defeat the Japanese was the task which faced him.

A week after landing in Delhi, with only a small personal staff, Mountbatten flew to Chungking to call on his neighbouring Supreme Commander, Chiang Kai-Shek. After four days of intense talks he flew back via parts of the Burma Front, finally visiting the Army/Tactical Air Force Headquarters for Burma set up at Barrackpore near Calcutta in one of the Viceroy's great houses, Belvedere. Here he met General Slim, Acting Army Commander, and Air Marshal Baldwin and the senior members of their staff. He was invited to address them, without any warning or preparation and not having discussed any policy with his staff or Commanders-in-Chief.

Entirely off his own bat, he made three points:

Generalissimo Chiang Kai-Shek with Mountbatten inspecting Chinese troops under SACSEA's Command. December 1943.

1. When the Japanese carried out their usual outflanking movements through the jungle his forces were to stand fast and not fall back on their supply lines. He would supply them by air.
2. He had heard that there were 120 men in hospital suffering from tropical disease to every one battle casualty. He was setting up a medical advisory team of tropical disease experts to deal with this problem.
3. He had heard that in the monsoon all active fighting stopped. The war would last twice as long at this rate. In future his forces would march on, fly on and fight on and gain the great advantage when the enemy expected both sides to stop.

After the talk Mountbatten flew back with the Army Director of Plans and asked what his colleagues thought of the speech. The reply was that they took a dim view of (1) as there were known to be hardly any transport aircraft; (2) would take a very long time to be effective and (3) only showed he had no notion of what the monsoon was like.

In fact (1) was a triumphant success as it stopped all further retreat, though Mountbatten had to divert American transport aircraft from supplying China 'over the hump', twice against President Roosevelt's orders. The improvement as a result of (2) was dramatic; within one year the rate of tropical disease cases had dropped to ten for every battle casualty, and (3) was the master stroke of the Burma Campaign and responsible for the ultimate Japanese rout.

Mountbatten's first offensive was to restore the morale of his men, which was at a very low ebb. He toured his whole Command to meet the men of all Services and of all nations. He would start off by gathering them round and saying: 'I hear you call this the Forgotten Front. I hear you call yourselves the Forgotten Army. Well, let me tell you that this is not the Forgotten Front, and you are not the Forgotten Army. In fact, nobody has even heard of you.' He would then go on: 'But they will hear of you, because this is what we are going to do . . .' and he would proceed to put them in the picture. As well as the pep talks, he obtained special broadcasts for the Forces on All India Radio. He demanded films for them, gramophones, theatrical shows, etc., and also arranged for SEAC news stories to be published in the British press. He set up their own daily newspaper called *SEAC*, later a weekly magazine called *Phoenix*, edited by Frank Owen who had been Editor of the *Evening Standard* before the war. After a while the men began to feel that people actually cared about them and this boosted their morale.

As Supreme Allied Commander, Mountbatten had the three Service Commanders-in-Chief under him. They, and his American Deputy, General Stilwell, were all a generation older than he was. For a Naval officer of forty-three, still some five years below the top of the Captains' list, though wearing the uniform of an acting Full Admiral, the situation was fraught with risks. His Naval C.-in-C. had been a Captain when Mountbatten was a Sub-Lieutenant. He had only to make one bad slip and his Commanders-in-Chief would be able to protest, which might have ended in his removal. However, his eighteen months' experience as a member of the combined British and US Chiefs of Staff gave him an insight into the conduct of the war at the top level which his Commanders-in-Chief lacked.

He took care to avoid General MacArthur's methods, of making plans with his personal staff without necessarily consulting his subordinate Commanders-in-Chief, who were then told to get on with them. He had to get their support. After some experiments, he decided that the Naval, Army and Air Directors of Plans should owe their single allegiance to the Commander-in-Chief of their Service, but that their joint allegiance for inter-service plans should be solely to him, and he met them regularly to ensure his views were well known. He had a real knack of talking to his senior officers and planners frankly and openly, inviting their views and criticisms. As a result of talking things out, he obtained general agreement as to what was the right and proper thing to do. He used to call it his 'Spirit of the Hive', where all were concerned to carry out the same plans in a way that was best for all, like Maeterlinck's bees. This spirit gradually pervaded the whole Command, through his frequent talks to Commanders on all levels and the other ranks and ratings as well.

Unlike Eisenhower, whose inter-service, inter-allied staff included US and British soldiers and airmen only, without a single Naval officer (other than one Public Relations officer), Mountbatten had a well-balanced staff of sailors, soldiers and airmen representing all the Allies. The formation of the Command Headquarters was therefore straightforward, but difficulties arose in regard to the control of the Naval, Land and Air Forces which took all Mountbatten's skill, tact and ingenuity to solve.

As far as the Land Forces were concerned, the position was complicated by the fact that the Deputy Supreme Allied Commander, Lieutenant-General Stilwell, US Army, had four differing responsibilities:

1. As Deputy SAC he was responsible to Mountbatten.
2. As Chief of Staff to the Supreme Commander of the China Theatre, his allegiance was to Generalissimo Chiang Kai-Shek who was, of course, independent of the Combined Chiefs of Staff.
3. As the Commanding General of the United States-China-Burma-India Theatre, he was responsible to the US Joint Chiefs of Staff.
4. As the Commander of the Northern Combat Area Command, he commanded the 1st and 6th Chinese Armies, and at the Cairo Conference in November 1943 Chiang Kai-Shek refused to let his large Chinese forces come under anyone other than the Supreme Allied Commander.

Various solutions were tried, but in 1944 Mountbatten became in effect the sole Commander of the Allied Land Forces in addition to being Supreme Allied Commander. This lasted until 12 November, when a new Land Forces Command was agreed to by the Allies and a new Commander-in-Chief took over the Land Forces from Mountbatten. The job had been no sinecure, since Mountbatten had had to settle matters such as inter-corps boundaries, the amount of tonnage allocated on the common lines of communication to the Central and Northern Combat Area Commands, and the other purely Land Force matters. He had to pay even more visits than usual to Stilwell's front.

Mountbatten shaking hands with Chiang Kai-Shek.

Talking to two army commanders General Liao (left) and General Sun Li Jen, 1944.

Relations with India Command were also complicated. The US Joint Chiefs of Staff had urged that India Command should be subordinate to the South East Asia Command. The British Government, however, decided it was constitutionally impracticable to place troops in India under a Commander not responsible to the Government of India. They further considered the two Commands were too large for one man to manage effectively. South East Asia Command therefore took over control of operations and India was left as the base for operational forces, both Commands remaining equal. It might well have been an unworkable proposition but for the goodwill between Mountbatten and his pre-war friend, General Sir Claude Auchinleck, the Commander-in-Chief in India.

Mountbatten made one of his greatest contributions to the success of the South East Asia Campaign in sorting out who was to control the Air Forces. He was so dissatisfied with the separate control of British and US Air Forces that on 11 December 1943 he issued a Directive of great political consequence. He turned the British Air Commander-in-Chief into an Allied Commander-in-Chief with all Air Forces under him. He grouped the RAF and US Army Air Force in Burma into a single integrated force under the US Air Commander. Great improvement in morale and efficiency resulted and ultimately it led to the creation of the independent US Air Force as it is today.

The effects of the new regime were soon felt throughout SEAC. Soldiers miserable in the grim weather conditions, cut off from home and falling like flies to unaccustomed tropical diseases, began to feel a sense of direction. Mountbatten's strategic orders from the Allied leaders were to prepare to attack the Japanese in Burma from their flank from the sea – an amphibious operation in which he was well fitted to succeed. With this in view he moved his headquarters to Kandy in Ceylon.

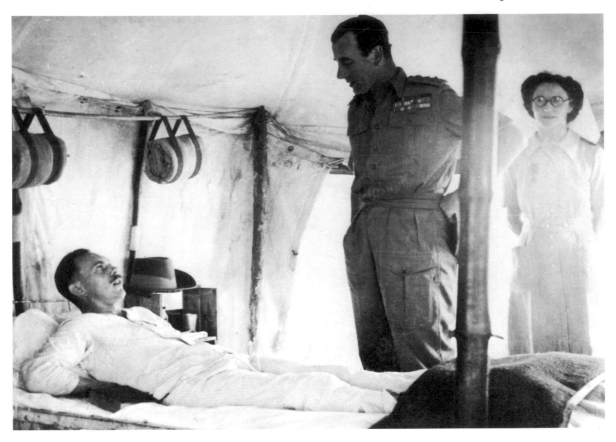

Visiting a wounded Chindit.

Talking to Royal Air Force units, December 1943.

The plan, as envisaged by Mountbatten, made use of large numbers of troops, ships, landing-craft and other equipment, which he had, but at the last minute the expedition was cancelled as practically all his landing-craft and landing ships were recalled for use in the invasion of France. This meant that the only way to attack the Japanese in Burma was by land advance from the North – an arduous undertaking, yet on it would depend the outcome of the war in South East Asia. The Japanese, at the same time, saw their next move as pressing on into India, so the two forces would meet head-on.

The Japanese struck first. In February 1944 they launched a diversionary attack on the 'Administrative Box' on the Arakan Front using their usual tactics of encirclement, which had worked so well until now on the badly supplied and demoralized British troops. But this time the British stood fast and held on for eighteen days. Mountbatten persuaded the Americans to let him take US aircraft from the supply route into China to use for supplying the cut-off troops at Arakan. When the relief columns arrived it was the Japanese who had run out of supplies, and they had to retreat with the loss of half their men. Field Marshal Lord Slim wrote that the battle of the 'Admin. Box' was the 'turning point of the Burma Campaign. For the first time a British force had met, held and decisively defeated a major Japanese attack.'

Speaking to air crew alongside a Mosquito, early in 1944.

On the Imphal–Tiddim Road, February 1944.

Opposite page: top
Mountbatten in procession with the Royal Family behind the gun carriage bearing the Unknown Warrior for burial in Westminster Abbey, 11 November 1920. King George V was chief mourner. Mountbatten walks between his father, Admiral the Marquess of Milford Haven, and Colonel Sir Clive Wigram. (Painting by Frank Salisbury.)

Opposite page: bottom left
The Sword presented with the Freedom of the City by the Corporation of London 10 July 1946.

Opposite page: bottom right
The Ceremonial Sword of Field Marshal Count Terauchi, Japanese Supreme Commander, Southern Regions, surrendered at Saigon on 30 November 1945.

Returning from visiting General Stilwell's front, Mountbatten was hit in the eye by a bamboo stump.

Visiting the battlefield of Kohima which British and Indian troops had resolutely defended. They had been buried where they fell. June 1944.

On 7 March 1944 on the Chinese front Mountbatten drove in his jeep over a bamboo stump which flicked up into his face. He received a severe injury to his left eye and was in No. 20 US General Hospital with both eyes bandaged when the Japanese followed their attack on the Arakan Front with a bigger attack by the 15th, 31st and 33rd Divisions, cutting off the 4th Army Corps on the Imphal Plain. Mountbatten

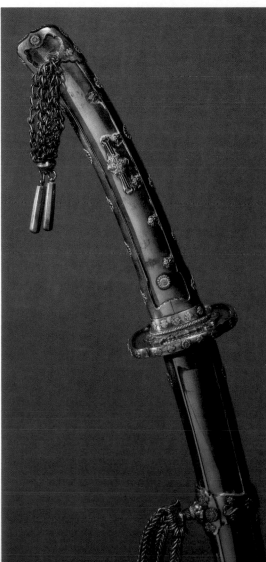

In the pilot seat of a US light aircraft before taking off for a jungle inspection tour with No. 1 Air Commando supporting Wingate's Chindits.

insisted on having the bandages removed from his eyes, thus risking losing the sight of his left eye, and flew on 13 March to the Army/Air Force Burma HQ at Comilla. Then and there he decided to move the 5th and 7th Indian Divisions from the Arakan Front to the Central Front by air and, as he had no spare transport aircraft, he took thirty off the American supply route into China against President Roosevelt's reiterated orders, and saved the Battle of Imphal. This was the first time in history that the ultimately responsible Commander had moved large forces from one front to another by air, and at a critical stage in a battle on both fronts.

In spite of Mountbatten's considerable success in getting additional transport aircraft from British and even more from US sources, there just were not enough to maintain the 14th Army by air in its thrust down the middle of Burma. Yet without this thrust Burma could never be liberated until more landing ships and landing-craft came back from Europe to capture Rangoon by sea.

The advancing troops needed nearly double the tonnage which the Air Forces could deliver at 'sustained rates'. Mountbatten solved the problem by calling on them to work at double these rates. The rates had been carefully computed as a result of long experience in both Air Forces and were only authorized to be exceeded for a few days at a time to meet a grave emergency. So he took a great risk in asking the Air Forces, flying and ground crews, to work at this terrific rate in the fearful climate and terrain of Burma for month after month.

The Air Forces responded magnificently. The Royal Air Force flew 196 hours a month instead of 100 and the Americans 204 instead of their 120, and the airlift rose to over 77,000 tons a month. Mountbatten never ceased to pay tribute to their quite fantastic effort, which he had called for and on which he had staked his career. He recalls the dangers of flights during the monsoon:

Lord Mountbatten photographed by Bern Schwartz.

'During the monsoon you get formations of cumulo–nimbus cloud which start down in the valleys and can in some cases rise to 30,000 feet – cloudbanks six miles thick. Inside these clouds an aeroplane could be hurled about and smashed to pieces. Often you could not fly over them. In the mountains it was extremely dangerous to try to fly under them. And often there was not enough fuel to fly round them. I often flew with our Air Forces during the monsoon, and I can remember very few more frightening experiences.'

Gradually the Japanese were beginning to get the worst of the war in South East Asia. Stilwell's Chinese and American forces captured Myitkyina, together with its important airfield. The Japanese fell back beyond the Irrawaddy and General Slim had to get his army across it by building boats out of the trees that grew along the bank. In January 1945 the 19th Indian Division crossed the Irrawaddy in two places north of Mandalay and succeeded in diverting Japanese troops from their real target, Meiktila, which was attacked by the 20th Division in February. Meiktila fell on 5 March and Mandalay was taken on 20 March. This was the climax of the Burma Campaign and Rangoon, the capital of Burma, was only 300 miles further on.

In April 1945 America and her Allies suffered a great loss. The President, Franklin D. Roosevelt, died in his third term of office. This came as a particular shock to Mountbatten. They had become personal friends in 1942 when he had stayed with Roosevelt at the White House and, as Supreme Allied Commander, Mountbatten had had a special relationship with him. The President had made this abundantly clear when he was appointed at Quebec.

Major General 'Pete' Rees, Commander of the 19th Indian Division, and Mountbatten after the capture of Meiktila, near Mandalay.

On the right of the photograph, Major-General Bill Donovan, Head of OSS.

Addressing US troops in 1944.

Showing Montgomery the position in South East Asia, August 1944.

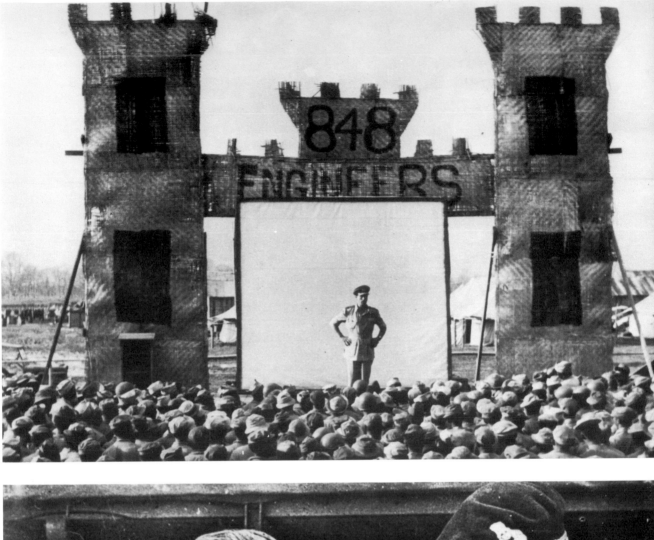

'General Eisenhower', the President said, 'is as much a servant of your King as of me. I trust you will feel the same way about me in South East Asia.' Mountbatten promised him he would be a good American and had always done his best to keep this promise.

On 7 May 1945 Germany submitted in 'Unconditional Surrender' to General Eisenhower. After five and a half terrible years of war, victory in Europe had been won. This was a marvellous tonic for the Allied Forces in South East Asia but their war was not yet over. They still had to defeat Imperial Japan. The 14th Army was nearing Rangoon but the monsoon was approaching and it was a toss-up which would win.

Mountbatten put into operation a double assault by sea and air. The main forces closed in up the Rangoon River and landed just outside Rangoon on 6 May and advanced on the city. The first entry into the city was made by amphibious forces. The prisoners of war in Rangoon jail had written on the roof 'Japs gone. Exdigitate.' Despite this welcome news, the Allied Forces carried on with the full-dress landing. They found that the Japanese forces had indeed gone and Rangoon was re-occupied without having to be bombed or fought over.

On 14 June 1945 he held an Army and Air Force Victory Parade, followed by a Naval Review. The men who had marched and fought for a thousand miles across some of the worst terrain in the world, had beaten the Japanese hands down and had overcome the monsoon and malaria, put on a splendid show.

After they had recaptured Rangoon, Mountbatten decided there was a need for closer co-operation with General MacArthur, who had his forces in the Philippines, so he went to visit him at his headquarters in Manila. Despite the fact that General MacArthur was twenty years older than Mountbatten and thoroughly autocratic in his methods of command, they got on well together and had no trouble in agreeing about future plans. But at that stage neither of them knew that their ideas were going to have to be very drastically revised.

On 17 July 1945, the last of the great inter-Allied Conferences of the war took place at Potsdam. Winston Churchill summoned Mountbatten to attend. Here he met the new American President, Truman, and Stalin. Immense decisions were taken at Potsdam, decisions which have affected the whole world ever since. It was here that Mountbatten first learned that the boundaries of his Command were going to be very greatly extended. He was also told the most closely guarded secret of the war; the story of the development of the atomic bomb. He was informed that an atomic bomb was about to be dropped on Japan and he was to prepare for an immediate Japanese surrender.

Steps were taken at once to launch Operation *Zipper*, the reconquest of Malaya, for which plans had been prepared many months earlier. All forces were sent to sea immediately after the bombs were dropped on Hiroshima and Nagasaki. They had to be diverted to the lee of the Andaman and Nicobar Islands and no landings were permitted until

General Slim and Mountbatten
talking to Commander Laurie
Durlacher. Penang Airfield,
September 1945.

General MacArthur had accepted the surrender of the Japanese in
Tokyo Bay on Sunday, 2 September 1945. That the landings would
have been a complete success was later confirmed by the fact that the
intelligence of the whereabouts of the Japanese forces proved to be
absolutely correct.

As areas of Burma were gradually liberated from the Japanese,
Mountbatten had to settle on a policy for the treatment of Burmese
collaborators. His Civil Affairs staff wanted to introduce severe
treatment, including flogging and the death penalty. When he heard of
this, Mountbatten replaced the Major-General in charge of Burmese
Civil Affairs and laid down that no one should be tried for
collaboration with the Japanese who had held the mistaken belief that
this would enable their country to attain independence after the war.
But crimes against recognized civil codes would be tried and
appropriately punished.

He announced that his Forces had come in friendship with the
Burmese to throw out their Japanese oppressors. He ordered his Allied
Land Forces Commander, General Slim, to make contact with Major-
General Aung San, leader of the 'Burma National Army' which had
been set up and controlled by the Japanese, and accept their transfer of
allegiance to fight under his orders.

This set the pattern for the future treatment of liberated colonial
territories, and after the Burmese had attained their Independence they
bestowed on Mountbatten their highest and very rarely given
decoration and title, Aga Maha Thiri Thudhamma.

Addressing 96th Royal Devon
Yeomanry Field Regiment RA,
near Klang, two days after they
landed at Port Swettenham,
11 September 1945.

On 5 September 1945 the Allied Forces reoccupied Singapore and
on 12 September, in the Council Chamber of Singapore Town Hall,
flanked by his senior officers, Mountbatten accepted the surrender of
680,879 Japanese in South East Asia in the presence of military
representatives of the United States, India, Australia, China, France
and Holland.

Mountbatten was determined that the Japanese should lose face and
insisted on senior commanders' swords being handed over in
Singapore and in all other appropriate places under his command,
whereas MacArthur forbad the taking of swords.

Mountbatten's opposite number, Field Marshal Terauchi, the
Japanese Supreme Commander, was suffering from a stroke brought
on by the news of the fall of Mandalay and so could not come to
Singapore. General Kimura, Commander of the Japanese Burma
Army in Singapore, surrendered to Mountbatten in his place and a few
months later in Saigon Mountbatten accepted two ceremonial swords

The Japanese surrender,
12 September 1945.

Mountbatten reading the Order
of the Day just after the Japanese
surrender. On Mountbatten's
right: General Slim. On his left:
the US Deputy SACSEA Lt
General R. A. Wheeler.

The Surrender Document.

The Supreme Commander, Japanese Expeditionary Forces, Southern Region, Field Marshal Count Terauchi, surrendering his ceremonial sword, forged in 1292. The case being surrendered with the sword signified that the Japanese did not expect it to be returned.

from Field Marshal Count Terauchi: one he presented to the King and the other, forged in 1292, he took home with him to add to his collection at Broadlands.

With victory in South East Asia came the problem of recovering and repatriating 125,000 Allied prisoners of war and internees. Mountbatten sent for his wife, who was Superintendent-in-Chief of the St John Ambulance Brigade and Chairman of its Joint War Organization with the Red Cross. She had already had a large hand in the recovery of Allied prisoners of war from Germany and so was quite an expert on the problem.

Mountbatten gave her a letter giving her authority in his name and putting her in charge of advanced arrangements for recovering prisoners of war and internees. Accompanied by only a small personal staff, she went from camp to camp, seeing the Japanese commanders and insisting that conditions were improved, and talking to the prisoners. Mountbatten went with her whenever he could. Many, who had been living below subsistence level for years, were only just alive and would have died without her intervention.

The legacy of the war in South East Asia was appalling. In every country the Japanese had invaded, administrations had broken down, there was poverty, sickness and fear. Mountbatten found himself responsible for a huge area – not only Burma, Malaya, Singapore, Siam and Sumatra but also, since the Potsdam Conference, the Dutch East Indies, parts of French Indo-China, Borneo and for a time Dutch New Guinea.

Mountbatten had to accept the surrender of nearly three quarters of a million Japanese soldiers, sailors and airmen. He had to feed 128 million starving people in the liberated areas as well as providing newspapers, radio news and police. There is no doubt that his wise and liberal policy set the pattern for the treatment of other colonial peoples and his policy was strongly supported by Clement Attlee, who had become Prime Minister in August 1946 immediately prior to the Japanese surrender.

One meeting took place that year which was to prove more important than Mountbatten could have guessed – that between the Mountbattens and Jawaharlal Nehru, the most prominent figure in the Indian Interim Government. In March 1946 Nehru came to Singapore to meet the Indian troops and study the conditions of the large Indian community. The local authorities wanted to ignore his visit, but Mountbatten lent him a car. He transported hundreds of Indian troops into Singapore to see Nehru and then drove with him through the streets of Singapore where they had a fantastic welcome. The Mountbattens had him to dinner at Government House where he was persuaded not to lay a wreath on the pro-Japanese Indian National Army Memorial. As well as preventing an outbreak of anti-British feeling, all this laid the basis of an enduring friendship between the Mountbattens and Nehru which was later to prove invaluable.

Mountbatten addressing Australian troops and hospital patients at 2/6 Australian Field Ambulance Hospital, Makassar, Celebes Islands, December 1945.

Driving from Guildhall to
Mansion House.

Receiving the Freedom of the
City of London. In Guildhall
Mountbatten was presented with
Nelson's Sword of Honour, 1946.

The Marshal of France, Juin,
investing Mountbatten with the
Grand Cordon of the Legion of
Honour at Les Invalides.

Mountbatten arrived in England to be showered with honours,
including a Viscountcy. On 10 July 1946, a month after the Victory
Parade, Mountbatten was presented with a Sword of Honour and the
Freedom of the City of London in Guildhall. He and Lady
Mountbatten drove through the streets of London in the traditional
open carriage amidst cheering crowds.

Allied countries also added their honours. At Les Invalides in Paris,
the Marshal of France, Juin, invested him with the Grand Cordon of
the Legion of Honour, and the Dutch gave him the Grand Cross of the
Order of the Lion of the Netherlands. The Chinese gave him the Grand
Cross of the Order of the Cloud and Banner.

Viscount and Viscountess
Mountbatten of Burma.

The Americans had previously honoured him with their Legion of
Merit in 1943 and in 1945 they awarded him the Army Distinguished
Service Medal, the first time a British Admiral had been so honoured.
Indeed, when President Truman was pinning the American Army
DSM on General Eisenhower at the Victory Celebration at the end of
the war, he declared he would sooner have this decoration than be the
President of the United States.

There was also the pleasure of being made First Freeman of the
ancient Borough of Romsey in Hampshire, where Broadlands is
situated, and of which he had been High Steward since 1939.

166

Everywhere there were cheering
crowds wanting to shake
their hands.

Receiving an Honorary Degree
at Oxford with Winston Churchill.

In 1946, Patricia married John the Lord Brabourne. Left to right: Pamela, Princess Margaret, Doreen Lady Brabourne, Viscount Mountbatten of Burma, the Queen, Lord Brabourne, the bride, the King, Viscountess Mountbatten of Burma, Mr Oliver Hoare, Princess Elizabeth and Squadron Leader Charles St John, DSO DFC (the best man).

In October 1946 Lord and Lady Mountbatten celebrated a great family event, the marriage of their eldest daughter Patricia who was twenty-two years old. She married her father's ADC, Lord Brabourne, whose father had been Governor of Bombay and Bengal and temporary Viceroy of India for six months in 1938.

Once again a Mountbatten wedding was attended by the King and Queen and this time their two daughters, Princess Elizabeth and Princess Margaret, were bridesmaids. Among the other guests was Mountbatten's nephew, Prince Philip, who was by now a Lieutenant in the Royal Navy and serving as an Instructor at the Petty Officers' School at Corsham in Wiltshire.

The bride with her father at Romsey Abbey.

As a crowning honour, Mountbatten received the most coveted award of all. The King created him a Knight of the 600-year-old Order of the Garter and his banner was hung in illustrious company in St George's Chapel at Windsor.

Mountbatten was just over forty-six years old and still in the Navy. He had just been specially promoted from the substantive rank of Captain to Rear-Admiral and badly wanted to get back to sea. He was told he would be appointed to command the 1st Cruiser Squadron in the Mediterranean Fleet after a Senior Officers' Technical Course at Portsmouth.

Instead he was given a task even harder, if possible, than the one he had just completed.

The Last Viceroy

THE Prime Minister, Mr Attlee, sent for Mountbatten and invited him to succeed Lord Wavell as Viceroy of India. His task was to transfer power to the Indian people.

But Independence for India was not just a question of handing over to a national party accepted by the majority of the population. Of her 400 million inhabitants – at that time about a fifth of the world's population – 250 million were Hindus, 90 million Moslems, 6 million Sikhs, and there were many other religious sects, including Christians and Buddhists.

Mountbatten was staggered by the Prime Minister's offer and did his very best to get out of accepting it. He finally asked to see the King, who as King-Emperor kept in close touch with Indian affairs. He pointed out to him that the chances of complete failure were very great indeed and it would be bad for him to have a member of his family fail. 'But,' the King replied, 'think how good it will be for the monarchy if you succeed.'

The British Government agreed to give Mountbatten a date by which Indian Independence was to be achieved: June 1948 – just fifteen months away.

Mountbatten did not want the job but he knew that to do it properly he could not send every proposal to the India Office in London for a decision, and he demanded full authority to act completely independently. This shook the Prime Minister who said: 'You are asking for plenipotentiary powers. No one has been given those in this century.' But after a long silence he said: 'All right, you have them.'

As Independence approached, the bitterness between Hindus and Moslems worsened. In 1946 it had erupted in the Great Calcutta Killings, when five or six thousand people were killed and 15,000 injured in riots, and violence spread to other parts of the continent. The war had also sharpened differences between the two communities. The Congress Party, the largest political party in India, had been weakened by its opposition to the war: Gandhi, Nehru and the leaders of the party, together with 60,000 of their followers, had been imprisoned by the British Government and, though the Party had claimed to speak for all Indians, disillusioned Moslems had by now transferred their allegiance to the Moslem League, founded in 1906 and growing steadily stronger. Its leader, Mohammed Ali Jinnah, was a fanatical supporter of the creation of a separate Moslem state – Pakistan.

Opposite page
Lord and Lady Mountbatten
in Coronation robes.

The Mountbattens arrived in Delhi on 22 March 1947 accompanied by their young daughter, Pamela. Two days later he was sworn in as Viceroy with all the majestic pomp and ceremony of the dying Raj. His only hope, he felt, was to establish friendly relations with as many of the Indian leaders as he could, so he set out to meet them one at a time and, to their surprise, he talked to them, not about the matter in hand but about themselves and their history. They had to understand each other if there was to be any hope of an agreement being reached between them.

The Governor-General of India, Earl Mountbatten of Burma in full dress uniform arrives with Lady Mountbatten for the 'Durbar' at the Palace of the Maharaja of Jaipur, December 1947.

Top
The Viceroy.

Bottom
The Mountbattens with their younger daughter Pamela, Viceregal Lodge, Delhi 1946.

The family at lunch with their Sealyham 'Mizzen'. Viceregal Lodge, Simla.

So when Gandhi arrived for his first meeting with Mountbatten, they talked for two hours about apparently minor things – Mountbatten's visit to India in 1921 with the Prince of Wales, his frustrated attempts to meet Gandhi, and Gandhi's own history and his non-violent Independence movement. Mountbatten realized that Gandhi's purely political power was lessening, though he still had an enormous influence on the ordinary people of India, who revered him as a holy man. His goodness and love of peace and his capricious, humble, sparrow-like personality endeared him to the Mountbattens. Their friendship soon grew and Gandhi started referring to the Mountbattens as his 'dear friends'.

Pandit Nehru was already a friend of the Mountbattens and he understood that the whole family loved India and would try to do what was right for his country. Sardar Vallabhbhai Patel was another vitally important figure. Inside the Congress Party he was as eminent as Nehru. He concentrated on internal politics and, as Home Minister, he controlled political appointments. He could be really tough and wielded great influence. At their first meetings Mountbatten and he

174

Gandhi, observing a day of silence, communicated with Mountbatten on the backs of envelopes. 2 June 1947. Part of what he wrote reads: 'I am sorry I can't speak; when I took the decision about Monday silence I did reserve two exceptions, i.e. about speaking to high functionaries on urgent matters or attending upon sick people. But I know you do not want me to break my silence. Have I said one word against you during my speeches? If you admit that I have not, your warning is superfluous.

'There are one or two things I must talk about, but not today. If we meet again I shall speak.'

The Viceroy and Vicereine's first meeting with Mahatma Gandhi, April 1947.

Tea with Gandhi. Gandhi, strict
in his diet, brought his own
goat's curds which he ate from a
tin bowl.

The Viceroy with Mohammed
Ali Jinnah.

With Jawaharlal Nehru
on an elephant.

had a stand-up row. Patel was used to getting his own way and he was
shocked to find that this was one person to whom he had to give way.
But give way he did and from then on their relationship improved and
they too soon became firm friends.

It was a different kettle of fish with Mr Jinnah, the Quaid-y-Azam
(the Great Leader) as his followers called him. To all intents and
purposes, Jinnah was the Moslem League and if any one man held the
future of India in the palm of his hand in 1947, that man was
Mohammed Ali Jinnah. Mountbatten adopted the same technique
with him that he had used for all the other leaders – using their first
meeting to get to know each other. This surprised Jinnah who after a
while relaxed but nonetheless remained cold. It was Jinnah who, more
than anybody else, made Partition inevitable. He would accept no
compromise.

The Viceroy and Vicereine
advance to meet rioting
Moslems, Peshawar, May 1947.

As he grew more familiar with India's mood, Mountbatten's hopes
for a united independent India receded. Soon after he arrived, violence
erupted in the North West Frontier Province and the Mountbattens
flew to Peshawar. They were greeted with the news that a huge crowd
of 70,000 to 100,000 Pathan tribesmen was about to march on
Government House. Mountbatten went immediately to the
demonstration and Lady Mountbatten insisted on going too.
Together, with no protection, they faced the enormous crowd, many
of them armed, who were waving the illegal green-and-white flag of
Pakistan and shouting 'Pakistan Zindabad'. The Governor told them
later that if the crowd had decided to march on Government House,
the local police and military could not have stopped them. But
something, perhaps the brave gesture of the Viceroy and his wife, or
the fact that he was wearing a green shirt as were most of the tribesmen,
turned the tide and the crowd's chant changed to 'Mountbatten

Zindabad'. For nearly half an hour the Mountbattens stood waving to the crowd – the noise was too great for any sort of speech – and eventually it dispersed.

Mountbatten's fears were now confirmed. Unless he acted very fast, the result would be a civil war of the worst kind. Any hope of handing over a united India had vanished. It was clear there would have to be Partition and this would have to come into being long before June 1948.

Working round the clock and using every ounce of tact, Mountbatten produced a plan that was acceptable to the Indian leaders. There were to be two Independent Dominions remaining within the Commonwealth: India, the vast majority of whose people were Hindu, separating Pakistan, West and East. However, he wished every Indian Province to vote on the plan in their provincial constituent assemblies. He would not personally take the responsibility of partitioning India. It had to be the Indians themselves who would ultimately take the decision.

On 4 June 1947 Mountbatten held a memorable press conference in Delhi and announced the solution for India. This was followed by a flood of questions and, in answer to one, he took his own staff completely by surprise by suddenly announcing that 15 August would be the date for the actual transfer of power to the two new Dominions. So now instead of fifteen months they had a matter of some ten weeks to complete the mammoth task, and a special calendar was put up in the Government offices and each day was crossed off as the transfer of power in India came nearer.

The official photograph of the Mountbattens celebrating their silver wedding, July 1947.

The Mountbattens with Indian Princes at the Silver Jubilee of the Maharaja of Jaipur.

One major problem was what to do with India's 565 ruling Princes who would now in theory become independent. They ruled over virtually a third of India and a quarter of its population with domains ranging from a one-cow pasture to a state as large as a Western European nation. As the King-Emperor's personal representative, Mountbatten had a special duty towards them, for they all had treaties with His Imperial Majesty.

Luckily Mountbatten knew a number of them well and some of them had been friends since his visit to India with the Prince of Wales in 1921. He saw the principal rulers separately, then summoned a full-scale meeting of the Chamber of Princes and persuaded almost all of them to submit to one or other of the two new Dominions in three areas in which the common interests of the countries were involved: defence, external affairs and communications.

Independence Day drew near. The astrologers had condemned 15 August as ruinously inauspicious, so it was decided that Independence should date from the stroke of midnight on 14 August. Rajendra Prasad, President of the Constituent Assembly, asked Mountbatten to become India's first Governor-General. He replied: 'I am proud of the honour, and I will do my best to carry out your advice in a constitutional manner.'

Prime Minister Nehru practising his daily yoga.

On 13 August the Viceroy, accompanied by the Vicereine, went to Karachi to install Mr Jinnah formally as the first Governor-General of the new Dominion of Pakistan. They had been told, during the ceremonies in Karachi, that there was a Sikh plot to throw bombs at Jinnah as he drove back in State from the swearing-in.

Mountbatten tried to persuade him to forego the State Drive altogether but Jinnah was determined to go, so Mountbatten insisted on accompanying him. They got back to Government House safely and Jinnah laid a hand on Mountbatten's saying: 'Thank God I've brought you back alive', and received the retort: 'Thank God I've brought *you* back alive.'

Back in Delhi, just before midnight on 14 August Pandit Nehru addressed the Indian Constituent Assembly. 'Long years ago we made a tryst with Destiny,' he declared, 'and now the time comes when we shall redeem our pledge, not wholly or fully, but very substantially. At the stroke of the midnight hour, when the world sleeps, India will awake to life and freedom.'

Mountbatten had accomplished his mission. He had transferred power within a sub-continent to 400 million people of many races and thousands of castes, speaking twenty-three languages and two hundred dialects. It was not the result he had hoped to achieve – that of handing over to a united India, but as events had turned out there was not the remotest chance of that.

As midnight struck in Delhi, Mountbatten sat at his desk awaiting the arrival of the Indian Leaders, Pandit Nehru and Rajendra Prasad, the President of the Constituent Assembly. At 8.30 a.m. on 15 August Mountbatten was sworn in as the first Constitutional Head of the new India.

Nehru and the Mountbattens.

Friday, 15 August 1947 was a great day in world history; it was a day of rejoicing in Delhi and all over India. Mountbatten's first act as Governor-General was to address the Constituent Assembly and then drive back to Governnment House amid vast crowds shouting 'Mountbatten Ki Jai'. The Mountbattens spent the afternoon with 5,000 school-children celebrating the day with snake charmers and dancing bears and other traditional Indian amusements.

But the rejoicing was short-lived. In Calcutta, Gandhi alone prevented a massacre by beginning a fast and threatening to continue to death if the communities did not end their strife. In the Punjab the story was sadly different. Despite the efforts of the 55,000-strong Punjab Boundary Force and others, massacres of Hindus by Moslems and Moslems by Hindus were causing terrible loss of life and dreadful destruction.

There was also a new problem – refugees. Moslems were trying to escape to Pakistan and Hindus and Sikhs were escaping to India. By 27 August it was estimated that some ten million people were on the move. At the beginning of September, the crisis in the Punjab had become acute and Delhi, India's capital, was almost in a state of siege. Mountbatten was in Simla when he received a telephone call urging him to return to Delhi where he persuaded the Indian Government, headed by Pandit Nehru and Sardar Vallabhbhai Patel, to set up an Emergency Committee. It was unanimously decided to invite Mountbatten to be its Chairman.

During this period, Lady Mountbatten devoted herself untiringly to work for the refugees and earned the undying love of the people of India. She drove herself very hard, going from camp to camp and hospital to hospital, often by plane although flying always made her sick. She knew very well the details of disaster – how to make sure inoculations were given, how many taps were needed per thousand people, how to attempt minimum levels of sanitation. She was not above moving a corpse that an Indian would not touch for caste reasons, and soothing the last moments of men dying of cholera in ankle-deep mud.

As the Emergency Committee, under Mountbatten's guidance, got to grips with its task, the violence was brought under control but there was a legacy of bitter resentment and desire for revenge.

The Government of India kindly allowed the Mountbattens to return to London for the wedding of their nephew, Philip Mountbatten, now created Duke of Edinburgh, on 20 November to Princess Elizabeth, the heir to the British throne.

When the great occasion was over the young couple accepted the Mountbattens' invitation to spend their honeymoon at their home, Broadlands, where the Mountbattens had started their married life back in 1922.

At the start of 1948 the sub-continent of India remained bitterly divided. Encouraged by Mountbatten, Gandhi once again threatened to fast to death to induce the Government of India to pay Pakistan her

Princess Elizabeth and the Duke
of Edinburgh on honeymoon at
Broadlands, 1947.

share of the sterling balance and to reduce communal violence. Again
the 'miracle' worked and Gandhi ended his fast on 18 January. Twelve
days later, on 30 January 1948, he was killed by a bullet fired by a
Hindu fanatic in the grounds of Birla House, Delhi.

Mountbatten takes up the tale:

'I had just returned from Madras that afternoon. First I heard
that there had been an attempt on Gandhi's life, and then, very
soon afterwards, that he was dead.

'To say that I was appalled conveys nothing – I was absolutely
numbed and petrified. I went round at once to Birla House. There
was a large crowd round the house already, and inside it most of
the members of the Government – everyone in tears.

At Gandhi's funeral, Mountbatten made all the dignatories sit in case the huge crowds pushed them on to the pyre.

'Gandhi looked very peaceful in death, but I dreaded what his death might bring.

'As I went into the house where his body was lying, someone in the crowd shouted out:

'"It was a Moslem who did it!"

'I turned immediately and said:

'"You fool, don't you know it was a Hindu?"

'Of course, I didn't know – no one knew at that stage; but I did know this: if it was a Moslem, we were lost. There would be civil war without fail. Thank God it wasn't! It turned out to be a Hindu extremist.

'What terrified me most now was the thought that these people might strike again – at Nehru, or Sardar Patel. There had been a growing coolness between these two great men. I took this opportunity, then and there, in front of Gandhi's body, of bringing them together again, as I knew he would have wished. They embraced each other in tears. I felt this act was a symbol of Gandhi's power, even after death. You still feel it strongly in India today.'

On 21 June 1948 Mountbatten handed over the office of Governor-General to C. Rajagopalachari, India's most venerable statesman. He and Edwina were fêted and cheered wherever they went in their last days in India.

On the eve of their departure, a farewell banquet was given to the Mountbattens and, in his speech, Pandit Nehru said: 'You came here, Sir, with a high reputation but many a reputation has foundered in India. You lived here during a period of great difficulty and crisis, and yet your reputation has not foundered. That is a remarkable feat. Many of us who came in day to day contact with you in those days of crisis learnt much from you, we gathered confidence and sometimes we were rather shaken, and I have no doubt that the many lessons we have learnt from you will endure and will help us in our work in the future.' He then went on to pay a glowing tribute to the work of Edwina and their daughter Pamela, and presented the family with a silver salver on behalf of the Cabinet and Governors of all the Provinces of India. This was engraved with all their signatures and inscribed: 'To the Mountbattens on the eve of their departure from India. With affection and good wishes and as a token of friendship.'

The Mountbattens give a farewell party to Government House staff, 19 June 1948.

The Mountbattens on holiday at
the Bay of Islands, New Zealand, 1946.

In February 1946 Mountbatten was in Australia where the Duke of Gloucester was Governor-General. Here Mountbatten is holding Prince William of Gloucester.

For his services in India Mountbatten had been created Earl Mountbatten of Burma but, when they returned home, he had to face from the reactionary and ignorant a chorus of disapproval. Churchill, who had given only grudging assent to the Partition plan, refused to speak to him. He was blamed by many for being in too much of a hurry, causing upheavals and loss of life in India. His answer to criticism was to say: 'History will be my judge.'

The Mediterranean and After

MOUNTBATTEN had made Attlee promise, when he accepted the Indian job, that when it was over he could return to the Navy. So in October 1948 he was once again a Rear-Admiral, commanding the 1st Cruiser Squadron in Malta. The ex-Supremo, ex-Viceroy, ex-Governor-General was now thirteenth in precedence on the island; in the Fleet he was under the command of people who had served under him in Asia. In 1950 the Commander-in-Chief Mediterranean wrote of him: 'Ordinary men can climb up with distinction: only extraordinary men can climb down without some loss of distinction. He has achieved the latter.'

In Malta he discovered a new thrill, skin diving with an aqualung, and during his time in the Mediterranean he spent many happy hours beneath the surface of the sea, even spearing a giant sting ray bigger than himself.

In 1949 he was promoted to Vice-Admiral. Despite his promise, Attlee did not leave Mountbatten alone, seducing him away from the Navy to a Cabinet appointment as Minister of Defence in the Labour Government, an approach which was to be repeated years later by a Conservative Government. In April 1950 he returned to the Admiralty as Fourth Sea Lord and Chief of Supplies and Transport. This was a nuts-and-bolts job, but unquestionably an imaginative appointment in the light of his probable future career in the Navy. The Supplies and Transport organizations in the Navy are not manned by uniformed personnel and Mountbatten worked closely with the Secretary of the Admiralty, Sir John Lang, and the Civilian Directors of Stores, Victualling and Armament Supplies. These departments had their own fleets and depots worldwide but – as a result of his wartime experience – Mountbatten felt that the link with the Naval Staff was not as close as it should be and the establishment of a Directorate of Administrative Planning was soon effected. This two years' experience of the civil side of the Admiralty was to prove of tremendous value to him ten years later when he set out proposals for the re-organization of the Ministry of Defence.

Victoria, Mountbatten's indomitable mother, now in her eighties, had been racked by arthritic pain for years, but living at Kensington Palace had kept an acute awareness both of the world – she was seldom without a book, which could range from a light novel to a solemn work on psychology – and of her innumerable relations and

A photograph by Baron of the Mountbattens at Broadlands in February 1947.

Overleaf
Commander-in-Chief, Mediterranean, 1952.

Overleaf: right
Dining with Emperor Haile Selassie of Ethiopia, Addis Ababa, January 1954.

descendants. She chain-smoked and had a dreadful cough, the only thing that could interrupt her autocratic flow of words: though in 1945 Mountbatten had noted, 'she now talks and coughs *at the same time*'. Her long life, which had seen so much history, was approaching its end and – when her health began to fail in 1950 – she returned to London from Broadlands where she had been staying. 'It is better to die at home,' she said. She hoped she would die quickly and was very cross when she lingered on and the relations who had already been to say goodbye to her had to come and see her for a second time. She would wake up in the morning and say: 'Am I still here? I'm not supposed to be here.' Death came at last on 24 September. Both the Mountbattens and her grandchildren felt her death acutely.

In May 1952 Mountbatten returned to the Mediterranean as NATO Commander-in-Chief, Allied Forces, Mediterranean. He had six Navies to co-ordinate: the French, Italian, Greek, Turkish and British Navies and some units of the American Navy, but he kept his the smallest headquarters of any NATO Command and raised Allied naval co-operation to a very high standard.

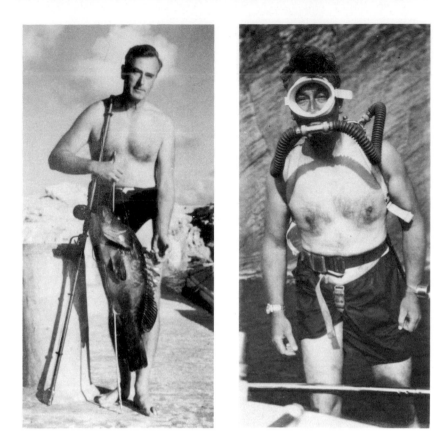

Straight through the nose!
Mountbatten with a large
Grouper, Malta, 1953.

Mountbatten is a skilled skin
diver. Gozo, 1953.

His tour of duty in the Mediterranean ended in 1954. As a parting
tribute, the six admirals representing the Allied Commander-in-Chief
formed a crew and rowed him to his flagship. His six years of return to
the Navy had been fruitful ones for him – he had progressed from
junior Rear-Admiral to Commander-in-Chief and was not only eager
to carry on up the ladder, but had also proved his fitness for it and his
devotion to his profession.

Prince Charles, aged 5, with his
great-uncle. Malta, February 1954.

Mountbatten and Prince Charles.

In June 1953 Princess Elizabeth, daughter of Mountbatten's cousin King George VI, was crowned Queen of England. After her marriage in 1947 to Prince Philip – Mountbatten's nephew – the Royal couple had come to stay many weeks with the Mountbattens in Malta when Prince Philip was serving in the Mediterranean Fleet. Princess Elizabeth and Princess Margaret had been playmates of the Mountbattens' two daughters, Patricia and Pamela, and he was very

Off on a Sunday picnic in
November 1949.

Previous page: left
Princess Elizabeth and the Duke
of Edinburgh at the
Mountbattens' house in Malta, 1949.

Previous page: right
Mountbatten and Princess
Elizabeth on the beach, Malta,
November 1949.

Opposite page
Mountbatten with some of his
family at Classiebawn, County Sligo.
Left to right: (back row) Lord
Brabourne, Lady Brabourne,
Lord Mountbatten, Lady Pamela
Hicks and Mr David Hicks;
(second row) Amanda
Knatchbull and Tania George;
(front row) Philip Knatchbull,
Nicholas and Timothy
Knatchbull, Edwina, India
and Ashley Hicks.

Overleaf: above left
Two keen photographers in flight.

Overleaf: below left
The Prince of Wales, talking to
his great-uncle after polo.
Windsor 1977.

Overleaf: below right
Princess Anne and Mountbatten
on board *Britannia*, photographed
by the Prince of Wales.

Overleaf: above, far right
The Queen, the Duke of
Edinburgh and Princess Anne
aboard *Britannia*, photographed
by Mountbatten.

Overleaf: above, extreme right
Prince Andrew and Prince
Edward aboard *Britannia*,
photographed by Mountbatten.

Overleaf: below, far right
Christmas 1977. Back row:
Norton Knatchbull, Lord and
Lady Brabourne, Lord
Mountbatten, Doreen Lady
Brabourne, Joanna Knatchbull,
Pamela Hicks, Michael John
Knatchbull. Front row: Amanda
Nicholas and Philip Knatchbull,
India Hicks, Timothy Knatchbull,
Edwina Hicks, Ashley Hicks, Mr
David Hicks.

fond of the young Queen. He became her personal ADC in 1953 and
felt closer to her than he had to her father or even her uncle, though he
had been personal naval ADC to both and a close friend of King
Edward VIII.

One of Winston Churchill's last acts as outgoing Prime Minister in
1955 was to appoint Mountbatten First Sea Lord. Churchill thus
became the only man to have appointed a father and son to the post,
and Mountbatten the only man to have followed his father in the job.
Mountbatten's dream of one day succeeding his father had come to
pass and he was glad that Churchill had overcome his animosity
towards him over what he had done in India.

He had so often been at daggers drawn with the Board of Admiralty
and had made the usual Navy jokes about its slowness and
conservatism. Now he was professional head of the Royal Navy and in
a position to be the butt of those jokes himself. He found it an
instructive experience.

Lady Mountbatten leaving
London Airport on her last tour,
18 January 1960.

Left: above
Five generations. The Queen
and the Queen Mother stand
with Lord Mountbatten behind
Princess Alice of Athlone,
Queen Victoria's granddaughter,
and Princess Anne with Peter
on her lap.

Left: below
Mountbatten with his
photograph album.

He had always been a reformer, but the particular reform he put into practice in 1955 was a new one for him: the Navy had to be trimmed and rationalized. Shore establishments had proliferated, while the new nuclear deterrent swallowed up much of the Defence budget. Mountbatten set up the 'Way Ahead Committee' to start things off and went round publicizing his aims. Personnel, uniformed and civilian, was cut by 30,000 and £15 million a year was saved, without losing a single ship from the sea-going fleet.

His other great aim was to bring the Navy up to date to fit the Service for its part in an age of nuclear power, computers and guided missiles. He introduced nuclear propulsion against much opposition mainly on grounds of cost. As always, fascinated by technology, he was keen to find practical uses for the latest discoveries.

This had been a feature of his whole career: Cockerell, the inventor of the Hovercraft, had only received Government backing because of Mountbatten's championship of his ideas and Mountbatten's own inventions had not been negligible. Some had been patented and adopted by the Admiralty. 'There was my sub-focal signalling shutter; my wireless wave-length calculator; my course ruler; the "M"-type torpedo sight – and the one I am proudest of, my station-keeping device, which would take far too long to explain, but which may be said to have saved my life, because I stood on it when the *Kelly* capsized at Crete, and I had to swim clear of the bridge!'

The changes in Britain's status since his father held his job had been staggering. From the greatest naval power in the world, she had become a poor country dependent on her alliances for defence. But she still had world commitments and the Services had to be designed to deal with tense situations that might arise. In July 1959 Mountbatten was appointed Chief of the Defence Staff and sweeping changes in the organization of the Armed Forces were on the way.

The year 1960 started happily for the Mountbattens with the marriage of their younger daughter, Pamela, to the interior designer David Hicks at Romsey Abbey on 13 January. It was like a fairy-tale wedding with snowflakes falling. Once again a Mountbatten wedding was attended by members of the Royal Family and foreign Royal relations, and Princess Anne was a bridesmaid. Edwina, or 'Lady Louis' as she was affectionately known by thousands, was in top form at the wedding – beautiful, gay and very happy. But she had been driving herself extremely hard, as she always did. The day after the wedding the Mountbattens went to Sandringham to see the Queen, who was expecting Prince Andrew, and a couple of days later Edwina set off on a tour of the Far East on behalf of the St John Ambulance Brigade and Save the Children Fund.

On Thursday, 18 February she arrived in North Borneo and the following day was a happy one spent in the country. On the Saturday she was far from well but with her usual determination and dedication to duty she insisted on carrying out her heavy engagements. This overtaxed what strength she had left and in the early hours of Sunday,

A happy family occasion was the marriage in January 1960 of Mountbatten's younger daughter, Pamela, to David Hicks, the interior decorator.

21 February 1960 she died in her sleep. The world mourned the loss of a great and courageous lady.

Mountbatten received the news by telephone in the early hours of the morning and simply could not grasp it. It was the greatest blow of his life. He received over 6,000 telegrams and letters many from Kings, Presidents and Prime Ministers but at least 5,000 were from ordinary people in all walks of life, who said they were great friends of hers and obviously knew and loved her.

One former infantry officer (the historian Christopher Hibbert) remembers an occasion typical of many which made Lady Mountbatten so much loved.

'I had been wounded towards the end of the war and was lying in hospital in considerable pain and feeling rather sorry for myself, when she came into the room. I remember her most clearly. She was wearing the uniform of the St John Ambulance Brigade. She sat down by my bed and I was immediately captivated by her presence which was very vivid without being the least obtrusive. She talked to me amusingly for quite a long time with a quiet easy, unhurried naturalness that was wonderfully refreshing. I did not feel up to saying much in reply, but I did say something which made her laugh, and when she had gone I felt so much better and, for the first time since being wounded, really quite cheerful.'

Her body was flown back to England and laid in Romsey Abbey guarded by estate staff on the spot where her daughter had stood to be married just six weeks before. Lady Mountbatten had asked to be buried at sea and the First Sea Lord at once offered a frigate, HMS *Wakeful*, and attended the funeral himself together with the Commander-in-Chief Portsmouth and all his senior officers. Prince Philip, in the uniform of Admiral of the Fleet, and his mother Princess Alice of Greece were among the family mourners.

The Indian Government insisted that one of their frigates, the *Trishul*, which was in England, should accompany her as her last Indian escort. India also further honoured her memory when both Houses of Parliament, the Lok Sabha and Raj Sabha, stood in two minutes' silence, the first time ever that any woman had been honoured in this way.

Mountbatten sought refuge in hard work. He turned his attention to a matter which had been in the forefront of his mind since the war – the need to reorganize the military machine in Whitehall and in Overseas Commands.

He foresaw that smaller forces would eventually be the order of the day and that a single Whitehall Ministry should be sufficient to administer them. But above all, his experience as Chief of Combined Operations and Supreme Allied Commander South East Asia had proved beyond a shadow of doubt that there was much to be gained in efficiency and economy by achieving far closer co-ordination in the three Services.

He was due to retire in 1962 but the Prime Minister, Harold Macmillan, persuaded him to stay on another year and see through the task of defence integration which he had already begun. Then the new Prime Minister, Harold Wilson, asked him to extend his time again.

He put up proposals for abolishing the three separate Service Ministries and placing these all together in a single unified Ministry of Defence under a new Secretary of State for Defence, with greatly increased powers for the Chief of the Defence Staff. This was an unpopular move among senior officers of all three Services but the value of it is now beginning to be recognized.

In July 1965, following his sixty-fifth birthday, Mountbatten retired from the Ministry of Defence. As an Admiral of the Fleet,

Mountbatten still remained on the 'Active List' but after fifty-two years he was no longer on active service duty. To mark his retirement, the Queen invested him with the Military Order of Merit and Mountbatten joined that august body of just over twenty men and women whose contribution in various walks of life is deemed to have been outstanding.

Earlier in 1965 he had been appointed Colonel of the Senior regiment in the British army, the Life Guards, with the responsibility for all matters of policy concerning the regiment, including interviewing new officers before they are commissioned into the Life Guards and approving appointments of senior officers before they are submitted to the Queen. He takes it in turn with the Colonel of the other regiment of the Household Brigade, The Blues and Royals, to do a spell of duty as Gold Stick-in-Waiting to the Queen, when he is required to accompany Her Majesty on certain State occasions such as the Birthday Parade on Horse Guards and the State Opening of Parliament, traditionally with the task of safeguarding her life.

That same year, 1965, he was also appointed Life Colonel Commandant of the Royal Marines. His family, including his nephew, Prince Philip, who is Captain General of the Royal Marines, have had a special interest in the Royal Marines since one of their ancestors, Prince George of Hesse-Darmstadt, personally led the Marines in their assault and capture of Gibraltar in 1704. As Chief of Combined Operations Mountbatten had been responsible for giving the Royal Marines amphibious craft to man and, when the Royal Marines Division subsequently came under his command, he converted them from Infantry to Commandos.

During their tercentenary in 1964, he presented the Corps with the music of the Preobrajensky March which they adopted as their Regimental Slow March. Mountbatten's uncle, Tsar Nicholas II, was Colonel-in-Chief of the Preobrajensky Guards and he gave the music to Mountbatten's cousin, King Alfonso XIII of Spain, for his Halberdier Guards. He in turn passed it on to Mountbatten and it was used as the theme music for the television series: *The Life and Times of Lord Mountbatten.*

A week after his retirement, he was installed by the Queen as Governor of the Isle of Wight, a post which had been held by his uncle, Prince Henry of Battenberg (Liko) who died on active service in the Ashanti campaign in 1896, and then by his widow, Princess Beatrice, Queen Victoria's daughter. He thus resumed a connection with the Island that had played a large part in his family's life and when in 1974 the Isle of Wight achieved County status, he was also appointed Lord Lieutenant.

With the 1965 festivities over, he went to his place in Ireland, Classiebawn Castle in the beautiful County of Sligo on the north coast of the Republic. Here, as in every year, he was joined by his family, which had considerably grown in size. His elder daughter Patricia and her husband Lord Brabourne have seven children, five sons and two

Of the many photographs of 'Edwina' this is the one Mountbatten loves the best and it goes with him wherever he travels.

Mountbatten with one of his granddaughters, Amanda Knatchbull, at Tidworth.

At Classiebawn, Mountbatten's Irish castle. Left to right: Amanda, Lady Brabourne, Joanna, Lady Pamela Hicks, Mountbatten.

Mountbatten presents the Rundle Army and Navy Cup to the Prince of Wales.

daughters, and his younger daughter Pamela and her husband David Hicks have two daughters and one son. Together they spent a happy, carefree month riding, fishing from his boat, *Shadow V*, searching for prawns among the rocks, or just playing on the sandy beach. It is here, perhaps more than anywhere else, that Mountbatten is able to demonstrate his unique capacity for bridging that 'generation gap' that seems to plague so many families.

Holidays over, he set to work on his many civilian interests. He made Broadlands his permanent base so that he could devote more time to his estate, including farming over 2,000 acres. He had, several years earlier, taken the unusual step of forming an Estate Committee to help run the affairs at Broadlands and this has proved a great success.

He is now involved with over two hundred organizations and was Executive Head or Patron of some sixty of these. At the end of the war, he had become Grand President of three Commonwealth-wide organizations, the British Commonwealth Ex-Services League, the Royal Life Saving Society and the Royal Over-Seas League and during his many travels abroad he uses every opportunity to strengthen the links between the peoples of the Commonwealth.

In 1964 he founded the National Electronics Research Council with the top people from the electronics industry, the learned bodies and institutions, universities and government departments. In 1967 it was reconstituted as the National Electronics Council with the express task of 'advising HM Government on the effects of electronics on our national way of life'.

In 1966 he accepted a two-year term of office as President of the British Computer Society and in October 1967 gave a major speech at the Guildhall on the importance of computers, about which he had first spoken in his Presidential Address to the Institution of Electronic and Radio Engineers back in 1946. That same year he was elected a Fellow of the Royal Society and served on their Scientific Information Committee and he also became a member of the Scientific Council of the Stockholm International Peace and Research Institute.

At the request of Prime Minister Wilson he headed an Immigration Mission to the countries of the Commonwealth. A year later the Home Secretary persuaded him to hold an enquiry into Prison Security. In less than three months he had produced his report and most of his recommendations were accepted and implemented. However, the Rabinowicz Committee turned down his main recommendation that there should be a maximum security prison on the Isle of Wight. He suggested that this would enable Category 'A' prisoners who were a threat to the safety of the country to be kept in more secure and humane surroundings without impinging on the rights of other prisoners of a lesser category. This, however, was turned down in favour of the 'dispersal system' which has not proved to be at all popular with the Prison Service itself.

Mountbatten has steadfastly refused to authorize any biography in his lifetime but after his retirement from active duty he was persuaded

THE CHARMER

N.Z.HERALD 5·6·47

"NOBODY WILL NOTICE
ANYTHING WITH THIS COVER ON"

DARK HORSE FROM DELHI

Mountbatten has always enjoyed
the cartoonists' views of his
career. Low and Minhinnick on
Mountbatten as Viceroy,
Cummings on Mountbatten at
fifty-four, Jon and Jak on
Mountbatten's report on Prison
Security in 1966 and Cummings
again on the effects of cuts in
expenditure on the Navy.

'Only been Viceroy of India and First Sea Lord!
Why, he's 54 and still got to make British Railways Chief, Prime
Minister and Director-General of Television.'

"WHAT YOU IN FOR, TOSH?"

THE SUPREMO LORD MOUNTBATTEN REVIEWS THE GRAND FLEET AT SPITHEAD

EVENING STANDARD - 2nd November, 1966

"Soon as he's past, start leaving at five minute intervals to avoid suspicion!"

Mountbatten takes a particular interest in the work of the United World College.

to agree to a television series of his life and times.

The twelve episodes took over three years to make and involved a tremendous amount of hard work, with Mountbatten spending hours in front of the camera telling his story and working with the producer, Peter Morley, and the historian, John Terraine. Mountbatten revisited locations in the Far East, Sri Lanka (Ceylon), Singapore, Malaya, Burma, India and Malta to film events where they had taken place. He was filmed in Churchill's War Room below the Cabinet Offices, attending a *Kelly* Reunion Dinner, on holiday in Ireland, and at Broadlands. Archive material, including actual newsreel shots both of the Mountbattens and events that had occurred during his lifetime, were included. The results were an instant success. The series was shown in over forty countries throughout the world. Mountbatten himself dubbed it into French and German and he was inundated with fan letters proving that his old friend Charlie Chaplin was wrong when he had captioned the photograph in his biography 'Breaking the news to Lord Mountbatten that he is no actor'!

In 1962 the Atlantic College of St Donat's Castle in South Wales was started as one of the most exciting and important experiments in international education in the world today. It was planned to set up international colleges around the world admitting boys and girls of ability and character regardless of nationality, background, race, colour or creed. They would spend the last two years of secondary education living, studying, discussing and adventuring together, and assisting the social services in the local community. An important part of this plan was to include teachers from other nations, who would come mainly on government teaching fellowships so that both students and faculty alike would discover common ideals based on loyalty and service to the international community. There were two aims: to encourage students and staff to return to their own countries convinced that international problems could be settled by reason and

210

discussion – not by war – and to meet new requirements for international education before university. To this end the project helped towards establishing the International Baccalaureate as the first international examination enabling students to enter all the major universities in the world.

Mountbatten had been unofficially involved with the Atlantic College and was instrumental in persuading the Royal Navy to release Rear-Admiral Desmond Hoare to become its first Headmaster. He later persuaded the British Government to give substantial grants to the College and in 1968 he accepted an invitation to become the project's first International President.

At that time there was only one College and no international organization although there were several people in different parts of the world who organized the selection of students and the financing of scholarships. Mountbatten set about visiting some twenty-five countries and persuading top-level people with an international outlook to form their own National Committees of which there are now over forty. He founded the International Council which comprises the Chairmen of the National Committees, and in many cases the Head of State accepted Mountbatten's invitation to be the Patron of the National Committee in their respective country.

He changed the name of the first College to the United World College of the Atlantic and in 1971 a second College, the United World College of South East Asia in Singapore, was opened by Prime Minister Lee Kuan Yew. A third College, the Lester B. Pearson United World College of the Pacific, was built on the southern tip of Vancouver Island in British Columbia as Canada's National Memorial to Mountbatten's great friend, Mike Pearson, who until his death was Honorary Chairman of the Committee in Canada.

In 1974 he visited the Chinese People's Republic for discussions with their Government about their further participation in the project. They have sent over twenty boys and girls and a teacher to the College in South Wales, a visit which proved to be an enormous success.

No sooner had Lord Mountbatten 'retired' than he embarked on an ambitious television history: *The Life and Times of Lord Mountbatten* with John Terraine and Peter Morley.

The Queen and Mountbatten in
the Condominium of
the New Hebrides.

Aboard *Britannia*, the Queen,
Prince Philip and Mountbatten.

A year later the Russian Government suggested that he should represent HM Government in Moscow at the thirtieth anniversary celebrations of the Victory in Europe. Here he took the opportunity to have discussions with the Russian Prime Minister, Kosygin, and his Minister of Education about the United World College project and as a result a Russian professor and a Russian boy were sent to the UWC of the Atlantic in South Wales.

His return to Russia after a period of sixty-seven years was an emotional time for Mountbatten. He had vivid memories of his time in the Kremlin back in 1908 and was able to pinpoint his nursery windows in the old Palais Nicholas. He then went on to Leningrad where he visited the Peterhof Palaces at Tsarsko Selo and the ruins of the little villa where the family had spent so many happy hours together near Peterhof. He went round the great Winter Palace in Leningrad and watched a performance by the Kirov Ballet from the same box that his uncle and aunt, the Tsar and Tsarina, had always used. He was treated with enormous respect by the Russians who were eager to hear his first-hand accounts of his Russian Imperial relations.

On 1 January 1978 Mountbatten was succeeded as President of the International Council of the UWC by his great-nephew, the Prince of Wales, and he was unanimously elected Life Patron of the project.

He had by now given up several of his other large organizations, such as the British Commonwealth Ex-Services League and King George's Fund for Sailors, which he had turned over to Prince Philip. It looked for a while as though he would at last settle down to a less hectic life, working on his extensive archives at Broadlands, visiting the Isle of Wight as Governor several times a year, going to London occasionally for duties in connection with the Life Guards, attending Naval or Royal Marine events or the occasional dinner in aid of charities such as Variety Clubs International, of which he is one of only three British Gold Card Members. But then he had a new idea. He would open his home, Broadlands, to the public.

One of the first examples of mid-Georgian architecture in England, Broadlands is a house with many royal and historic associations. Romsey Abbey had owned the manor since before the Norman Conquest but surrendered it to Henry VIII after the Dissolution of the Monasteries.

Edward VI granted it to his uncle, Admiral Sir Thomas Seymour, who sold it to Sir Francis Fleming in 1547. His daughter married Edward St Barbe and it remained in the St Barbe family for over a hundred years. In 1736 the home was sold to the Palmerston family and, at the request of the second Viscount Palmerston, 'Capability' Brown, the famous architect and landscape gardener, began to transform it into the beautiful building it is today. Henry Holland the Younger made 'further alterations' in 1788 and Robert Adam is believed to have supervised much of the rich interior decoration work.

Lady Mountbatten was a direct descendant of Palmerston and the house has always been greatly loved by the Mountbatten family. It is typical of Lord Mountbatten that he should wish people to have the opportunity of getting to know the house which has meant so much to him.

Epilogue:
The Man and his Achievement

To Lord Mountbatten
In grateful remembrance
of a letter he wrote me
45 years ago and
which contained the
suggestion of an idea
for a book which I
subsequently embodied
in the book entitled
"The Murder of Roger Ackroyd"
Here with once more – my
thanks –
Christmas 1969
Agatha Christie

Agatha Christie acknowledges in this dedication Mountbatten as the source for the idea behind *The Murder of Roger Ackroyd*, her most famous detective story.

Broadlands

LORD MOUNTBATTEN emerges from any recital of the events in his life as predominantly a man of action, and capable of provoking the action he wants in others: a leader. But leaders have to know where they are going, and he has always displayed a brilliant analytical mind, quick to sort out the pros and cons of any question and come to a decision, usually the right one.

Mountbatten's 'congenital weakness for thinking I can do anything' – his own words to Churchill – has never made him an autocratic leader. He is a believer in discussion, in asking people what they think, taking expert advice and then making up his mind. This ability was nowhere more important than in India when, as last Viceroy, he had the almost superhuman task of resolving the Indian dilemma without precipitating a civil war.

In the Royal Navy and in other positions of authority it would often have been enough for him to have used his commanding presence and ability to make rapid decisions to steam-roller his ideas through and put the rusty wheels of bureaucracy into movement. But Mountbatten always preferred to win the whole-hearted support of the people he was directing and instil in them a spirit of keenness and willing co-operation.

The men of the *Kelly*, after she had been all but sunk, flocked to rejoin her as soon as it was possible and, when she finally did go down in the Battle of Crete, the survivors organized a unique commemorative association with regular reunion dinners, so highly did they value the experience of being part of a very special team.

The ability to drive himself – and others – very hard, to do without much sleep, to work every hour of the day, is part of Mountbatten's secret. If genius is ninety per cent application, he certainly has it. This drive is an integral part of his character but also stems from his position as a member of the Royal Family.

Twice in his Naval career this led superiors to ask for somebody else when they learnt that he had been assigned to them and both times he triumphantly proved them wrong. In that most professional of Services, the Royal Navy, Mountbatten proved himself and his appetite for hard work; his wide-ranging mind and eye for detail were particularly valued during the war years. (He is the only member of the Royal Family to have fought in both wars.) He was of course outstandingly successful as Supreme Commander in South East Asia,

Vice-Admiral, Earl Mountbatten of Burma playing polo for Hampshire against Hertfordshire. Roehampton, 1950.

inspiring that 'Forgotten Army' with the will to win, but it must not be forgotten that he also played an important part in planning the invasion of France which led to the winning of the war in Europe.

The desire to be at least twice as good as the next man was apparent early in his life and owed something to the pride he felt for his father. Prince Louis of Battenberg had reached the top of his profession – First Sea Lord – by exhibiting a combination of abilities very like Mountbatten's. Father and son had much in common. Mountbatten's mother sometimes noticed uncanny resemblances between them, such as the tendency when very tired to 'relax' through turning to a different kind of hard work. Thus, in India, Mountbatten found relief from the intolerable pressures of the job in complex genealogical research (later becoming President of the Genealogical Society). Reaching the position his father had held, First Sea Lord, was a symbolic victory, but one which meant a great deal to him.

216

The strongest emotional experiences in his life – his father's resignation, the massacre of his cousins, his marriage – necessarily have intimate connections with the official self, but they are kept more or less out of sight. The brutal death of the Imperial Family, so terrible that too little remained of their bodies for burial, underscored his revulsion against unnecessary violence. This refusal to use blunt force was especially evident during his time in South East Asia clearing up the chaos left by the war. The war itself he saw as a just war of democracy against dictatorship but he never forgot the men who risked their lives in achieving this end. It was typical that he should refuse to countenance revenge attacks on those in Burma and Malaya who had used the Japanese invasion to further their own national struggles, and this example was followed by the British Government in their treatment of other colonial peoples.

Lord and Lady Mountbatten shared a deep and genuine concern for ordinary people which few would have suspected in the Twenties, when news of the Mountbatten 'smart set' filled the popular press as a welcome diversion from the realities of the Depression. Mountbatten has always had, again like his father, a knack for winning the affection of the lower deck through his practical interest in them. Edwina Mountbatten showed the same qualities, and her devoted service to the St John Ambulance Brigade and to all the sick and desperate people with whom she came into contact during the war and in India endeared her to many thousands. She was an invaluable support to her husband in every job he took on, especially in India.

Brilliance, decisiveness, hard work and humanity add up to a formidable picture. But they are all general qualities that could have been applied in fields other than those he chose. During his years in the Navy – and to him they are the core of his professional life – Mountbatten was also able to develop his particular bent for inventions and technology. In an undergraduate revue he was once depicted as saying 'I invented technology'. His father before him had shown the same talent, with his 'Battenberg Course Indicator'; Mountbatten's equivalent was the 'Mountbatten Station Keeping Equipment'. His interest in such diverse activities as flying, education, cinema, cypher machines, supporting in many instances improvements and innovations long before the official bodies countenanced them, is typical of his restless enquiring mind.

The story of Lord Mountbatten's unique and extraordinary career remains to be told but the photographs in this book provide a glimpse of eighty highly eventful years.

Bibliographical Note

FOR readers interested in Lord Mountbatten's career, there are several excellent books, including *The Life and Times of Lord Mountbatten*, an illustrated biography based on the television series, by John Terraine (Hutchinson 1968). In this very successful series Lord Mountbatten told some of the stories he tells here, in greater detail.

There is also Richard Hough's biography *Louis and Victoria* (called *The Mountbattens* in the United States). This, as the title indicates, is mainly about Mountbatten's parents but also covers Mountbatten's early career (Hutchinson 1974 and Dutton 1975).

Kelly by Kenneth Poolman (William Kimber 1954) tells the exciting story of that brave ship and *Freedom at Midnight* by Larry Collins and Dominique Lapierre (Collins, and Simon and Schuster 1975) describes the gaining by India of its Independence and Lord Mountbatten's part in it.

Acknowledgments

FRANK Salisbury's painting of the Unknown Warrior on page 153 is reproduced by gracious permission of Her Majesty the Queen. Permission to reproduce the following photographs and pictures is also gratefully acknowledged: Associated Press for the photograph on page 173 of the Mountbattens attending the Durbar of the Maharaja of Jaipur in 1947; Camera Press for the photographs of Lord Mountbatten on page 207, Lord Mountbatten and his granddaughter Amanda Knatchbull on page 206 and the Prince of Wales and Mountbatten on page 207 and also for the colour photographs by Lord Kilbracken of Lord Mountbatten (frontispiece) and Lord Mountbatten with his family on page 197 and Arthur Edward's colour photograph of the Prince of Wales with his great-uncle on page 198; the *Daily Mirror* for the photographs of Prince Charles and Lord Mountbatten on pages 192 and 193; the Imperial War Museum for the photograph of Admirals Wemyss and Beatty on page 49; the Press Association for the colour photographs of five generations of the Royal Family on page 200; HRH the Prince of Wales for the colour photographs of Princess Anne and Lord Mountbatten on page 198 and of Lord Mountbatten taking *his* picture also on page 198; Carlos Sancha for the portrait of Lord Mountbatten on page 19; Bern Schwartz for the colour photographs of Lord Mountbatten on page 154 and the photograph of Broadlands on page 215; Sport and General Press Agency Ltd and Barratts Photo Press for the photographs on page 169 of Lord Mountbatten and his daughter Patricia after her wedding, the photograph on page 183 of Princess Elizabeth and the Duke of Edinburgh on honeymoon at Broadlands and Lord Mountbatten after polo on page 216. The cartoons on pages 208 and 209 are reproduced by permission of the *New Zealand Herald* (Minhinnick), the *Daily Mail* (Jon) and Express Newspapers (Low, Cummings and Jak).

Index

(Earl Mountbatten of Burma has not been included in the index)

The Coronation Procession of King George VI and Queen Elizabeth, 12 May 1937. Commander the Lord Louis Mountbatten rides behind HRH the Duke of Gloucester and HRH the Duke of Kent and between Major-General the Earl of Athlone and Colonel the Earl of Harewood.
(Painting by Frank Salisbury.)

MOUNTBATTEN'S DESCENT FROM QUEEN VICTORIA
(Showing Sons' Children)

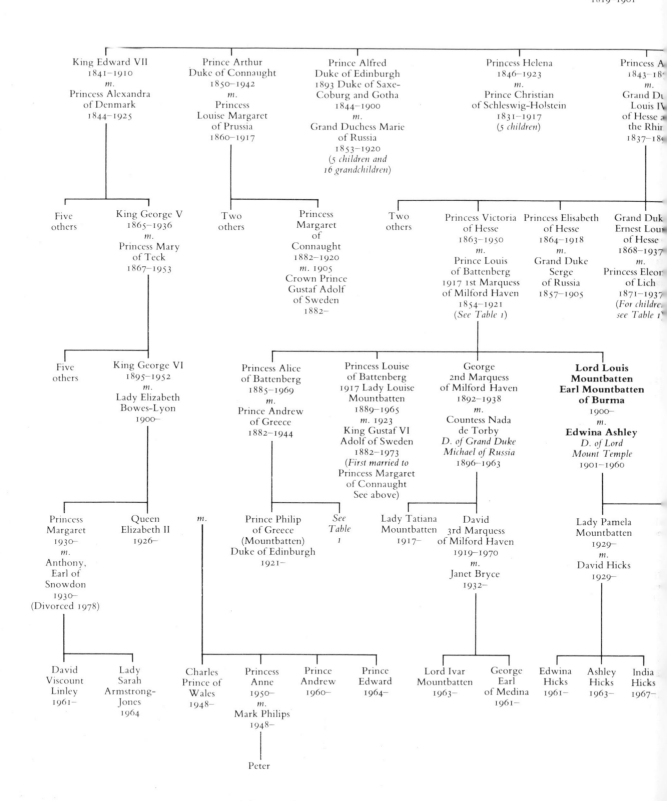